Yankee Doctor
in the Bible Belt
a memoir

SEEDS
HARDWARE
MEDICAL CLINIC
Main St.
JOE'S DINER
LIBRARY
WWI
DRY LICK
est. 1870
Pop. 2000

Janet Tamaren, MD

Yankee Doctor in the Bible Belt
a memoir
© 2021 by Janet Tamaren, MD.
All rights reserved.

Although the name "Dry Lick" is fictional
and the names of patients have been changed
and details of their lives obscured,
these stories are all based on real people.

Book Consultant: Judith Briles, The Book Shepherd
Editors: Peggie Ireland, Nina Synder, and Judith Briles
Cover Illustration: Risa Aqua
Cover, Interior Design, and eBook conversion:
Rebecca Finkel, F+P Graphic Design

Books may be purchased in quantity
by contacting Caduceus, LLC directly at
www.JanetTamaren.com

Library of Congress Control Number: 2021900627
ISBN trade paperback: 978-1-7356199-3-4
ISBN eBook: 978-1-7356199-4-1
ISBN Audio: 978-1-7356199-5-8

MEMOIR | MEDICAL | APPALACHIA

First Edition
Printed in the USA

To Lauren—

My friend who helped me get through medical school;
who shared innumerable cups of coffee with me,
as we discussed patients who had amused us
or scared us or touched our hearts in some way.
She always had strong opinions, as well as a kind heart.

Author's Note

In medical school, I was taught what was called factoids; thousands of small facts about pathology or anatomy. During my internship, I learned to function with chronic sleep deprivation, usually working 80 hours per week. During school and subsequent years of training, instructors talked about the "steep learning curve."

The steepest learning curve started, though, when I finished training and got catapulted into the world of working as a physician. That was when I learned the real craft of doctoring. This memoir details the joys and tribulations of day-to-day doctor life.

I learned how taking care of patients was almost a sacred trust. They taught me about courage, perseverance, heartbreak, and life not to mention the intricacies of medicine: the challenges and mysteries, and puzzling patients.

I grew up in a suburb of Cleveland, Ohio. I went to medical school in Kentucky. Although the two locations are only a physical distance of three hundred miles, the two states are thousands of miles apart in culture and history.

After training, I went to work in a small town in rural Kentucky. The state had four traditions that make it a culture unto itself.

- For one thing, it has its own dialect. They speak English with an accent and with idioms unlike anywhere else in the country.

- Second, it has an intuitive mistrust of outsiders—like people from New York City, a location which was described in the local paper as the devil's playground.

- Third, it boasts strong family bonds. Southern folk stay close to their roots. They visit parents or grandparents frequently, or even live next door to them. They do not choose to move away from home.

- Fourth, it has strong religious beliefs, often evangelical or fundamentalist Christianity.

I am including, besides medical stories, impressions of the rural south, from the point of view of a Yankee from Ohio. That's me. To that end, I have also added a few comments on the culture and history of Appalachia.

The town I practiced in consisted of a main street with a courthouse. My medical practice shared a building with a video rental store. Other businesses in town were two restaurants and a hardware store.

I have given the town the fictional name of Dry Lick. All names and identifying features of patients have also been changed for privacy.

— Janet Tamaren, MD

contents

early days in practice

I had become Alice in Wonderland
who had wandered into a strange land.

I had finally finished my training. I was done with the Big City Hospital and the 80-hour weeks as a resident. I could pick up the pieces of my life at home and maybe see my children on a regular basis. Accepting the position as a physician in a rural community that required an hour-long drive from where I currently lived became a treat—no calling *Dr. Tamaren* on the overhead paging system that blasted through the hospital. The peace of the countryside was a gift.

Now, I was a child of the suburbs. The first day I commuted was a bit scary. I took a road off the highway. The road followed a river that cut a deep swath through the trees and foliage, which only seemed to get thicker. I persevered. That is, I kept driving.

Eventually, the woods lightened up and open land lay before me. Then a town appeared, a welcome sight, complete with a county courthouse.

I soon discovered that Dry Lick boasted a population of 2,000 people. This tidbit of information was gleaned from the sign I drove past, as I entered the town.

Dry Lick had two main roads: Broadway and Main. My arrival revealed two more; it even had two restaurants. There used to be a Dairy Queen, but it burned down. The lack of a Dairy Queen, it turned out, was a real bummer. Most small towns in Kentucky had a Dairy Queen if nothing else. I would soon crave it.

My target awaited me: a modest rural hospital with an attached, equally modest clinic, very modest. After parking my car, I introduced myself to the staff: an office manager, a receptionist, and a nurse. Greeting each, I donned my white doctor coat, wrapped my stethoscope around my neck and saw my first patients, one of whom was not terribly reassuring. I felt I had become Alice in Wonderland who had wandered into a strange land.

coon hunting

Aha! A clue! I feel like Sherlock Holmes.

A child of eleven or so sits in the exam room with his father. The child is a sturdy young boy, with the gentle twang everyone has in the state. The father is a bit rough around the edges, wearing a well-worn flannel shirt, well-worn blue jeans, and muddy boots.

"He ain't staying awake at school. Teacher says he keeps on falling asleep. I don't have no idea what's wrong. Mebbe he is sick or something," the father says.

School just started in early September. The boy, when I look him over, doesn't look sick. His color is good. He is alert and bushy-tailed, except maybe a bit tired-looking.

"You been sleeping okay?" I ask the boy. "Yep." I probe further, in my highly trained manner, "Do you have any idea what makes you fall asleep at school?"

This is a subtle question. My past years of schooling have taught me to look for subtle findings. Maybe he has a seizure disorder, *petit mal* seizure, that makes him blank out at times. Maybe he has narcolepsy —a neurological disease that can make a person fall asleep at odd times, like the middle of the day. Maybe he has juvenile diabetes.

"I just get sleepy," the boy says, which does not help at all. Instead, I approach this diagnosis indirectly. "What time do you get to bed at night?"

"Well, first I go coon hunting after dinner. Then I get to bed," he replies. This does not tell me much. I didn't know what "coon hunting" means. I probe further. "What is coon hunting?" I ask.

I didn't know what coon hunting was.

This earns a look of disbelief on the boy's face. He can't believe that I don't know what coon hunting is. He explains it to me.

"Well, you take your rifle, and you go out in the woods, hunting for coons." This is extremely enlightening. Eventually I figure out the word I am searching for is "raccoons." Part one of a mystery is solved.

"How long do you go out for?" I ask.

"Might take two or three hours. The moon is out the last few nights, so I stay out longer than other times," he says.

Aha! A clue! I feel like Sherlock Holmes. "So, what time would that be?" I ask.

"Mebbe one in the morning, I reckon, before I get back inside the house," he says.

The father looks untroubled by this information. It doesn't bother him in the least that his 11-year-old son is out coon hunting until one in the morning.

I then proceed, with my keen intellect, to the critical question. "And what time do you have to get up to go to school the next morning?"

"I get up at 6 a.m., what with needing to catch the bus at quarter 'til seven," he says.

I have successfully figured out what coon hunting means.

I narrow down the differential diagnosis. This child might get all of five hours of sleep at night. This explains him falling asleep at school.

I explain my logic to the child and his father, mostly to the father. The boy is completely untroubled by his tiredness. I tell the father he has to cut back on his coon hunting or else the school is going to get angry and cause the family some problems. His son needs more than five hours of sleep. I suggest a bedtime around 9 or 10 p.m. This will allow at least eight or nine hours of sleep.

The father takes this information in hand. He also takes his crumpled hat in hand. I write a note to the school, saying he is just sleep-deprived and should straighten up in no time at all. Whether they pay me any mind or not, the coon-hunting season is almost over.

So that solves the Case of the Sleepy Child. What with four years of medical school behind me and additional years of specialty training at the fancy tertiary-care hospital, I have successfully figured out what coon hunting means.

mountain dew
I don't drink no Coke.

In another month or so, another patient I see has a similar complaint of sleep problems. I enter the exam room and meet Ms. Misty. She is a pretty 24 year old, but she looks a bit peaked.

"I ain't been sleeping," she says. "I cain't fall asleep at night. I don't know what's wrong with me. Mebbe I need a sleeping pill."

Ms. Misty is perky enough that she has on her makeup: thick eyeliner, mascara, some blush for her cheeks. She is wearing a summer outfit thatis a bit brief. Perhaps she shows a bit more cleavage than the usual patient. I mention this because of what she tells me next.

She reveals she works as an exotic dancer and works late at night. When she gets home, maybe at 2 a.m., she has trouble falling asleep. Ms. Misty adds that she might get three hours of sleep at night.

I ask her how much coffee she drinks.

"I don't drink no coffee," she says. I ask her about other sources of caffeine, such as Coke. "I don't drink no Coke."

Eventually, after other probing questions, she mentions that all she drinks is Mountain Dew. I ask, "How many bottles or cans a day do you drink?"

"Six or seven," she says.

Another "Aha!" moment on my part. Mountain Dew is chock-full of caffeine,

To my relief, it turns out that my medical acumen is sharp.

whether she knows it or not. I explain this to her and encourage her to cut way down on the Mountain Dew and see if that doesn't help with her problems falling asleep. She agrees to give it a try, although she does sound cynical, and not entirely convinced that I am right. After all, everybody in town drinks Mountain Dew.

To my relief, it turns out that my medical acumen is sharp. I see her for a follow-up visit. She cut back on Mountain Dew. She continues exotic dancing, but she can sleep at night after her shift at the club. The Case of the Sleepy Young Woman is successfully closed.

couch on fire
She had bedbugs.

As part of the steep learning curve in the small town where I serve as a doctor, I learn many things. One of them is how NOT to treat bedbugs.

As I drive into town one morning, I see that a building along the town square is on fire. Fire trucks scurry everywhere. The staff tells me an apartment building has gone up in flames. The nursing staff is heading off to the burning building, bringing water bottles to the beleaguered firemen. There is smoke wafting across the county courthouse lawn of the capitol. The smoke drifts in the direction of the clinic, marring an otherwise bright August day.

We hear that a few people had gone to the ER for smoke inhalation and other injuries. By the late afternoon, the fire is extinguished. The building is totaled, but the surrounding structures are saved.

The rumor mill is buzzing. We hear that the fire started on a resident's couch. She had bedbugs in her couch. She took gasoline and poured it on the couch. She thought this would kill bedbugs. Unfortunately, she is a smoker, which is not unusual in Dry Lick. Half the town are smokers. Somehow, the couch caught fire. We do not get any further information regarding the bedbugs, whether they survived or not. I think not.

I meet the perpetrator a few days later. She comes into the clinic, complaining of low back pain. Apparently, she fell down the stairs as she fled the burning apartment. Her injuries are not serious. Almost everyone in town is mad at her. The building got rebuilt, and life went on in Dry Lick.

what this taught me:
Do not use gasoline to kill bugs on a couch,
especially if you smoke.

CHAPTER TWO

settling into the practice

I get to know my patients and other strays in town.

I settle into the practice. I still feel like a stranger in a strange land. The locals do not help. I look like I am from the Mediterranean, with my olive complexion and curly dark hair. A patient asks what country I am from. He says I look like I am from another country, plus I talk funny. I tell him I am from Ohio.

"Aha! I knowed you was from another country!" he says with dead seriousness. As it turns out, many folk in town have never been farther than twenty miles away in their entire lives. So, this person's ignorance of boundaries and geography is not that unusual.

After a while, I understand pretty much what people say. The residents of Dry Lick play fast and loose with their vowel sounds and how many syllables can be invested into a word written with a single syllable. For example, "dead" becomes "day-ed" in their sentences. I become accustome to waitresses saying, "Here you go, sugah" when they deliver my meal. Everyone, male or female, is called "sugah" as a default position.

But all in all, I get to know my patients and other strays in town. Sometimes I feel I could even help someone in need, often a teenage mother. Teen pregnancies are not all that unusual in rural Kentucky. Often, the teen's mother takes in the baby and raise him or her.

dixie and the baby

*The new mother, a child herself,
with a minimal support system.*

I first meet Dixie in the clinic: a girl of fifteen with a one-week-old baby on her lap. Dixie says she is here because they told her the baby needs a repeat blood test. She does not look worried; she mostly looks tired. And she keeps baby Matthew some distance from her body. She holds him like a bag of potatoes on her knees.

As a first impression, it looks like she isn't bonding to the baby. Usually, a new mother holds a newborn right up against her chest. She is not doing any of that skin-to-skin contact. This is worrisome.

The clinic staff, of course, *ooh* and *aah* over the baby and take turns holding him. We all have children. We always respond this way to a baby. We try to model for Dixie how much a baby likes to be cuddled.

I talk to Dixie asking who lives with her, and if she has help with the baby. Dixie tells me that she lives with her boyfriend and she is a freshman in high school. She does not mention a mother.

Dixie and her baby are sent to the nearby hospital to get the repeat blood test that all newborns get. At the same time, we ask Dixie to come back in one week for follow-up.

My clinic thinks about calling Social Services to alert them that the baby is at some risk. If the mother fails to bond to the baby, the baby can develop failure to thrive that can be deadly. It turns out that Social Services already knows about her situation and were being supportive. We continue to see her and the baby fairly frequently. The second visit, she holds Matthew closer to her. By the third week, she cuddles him. Thank God.

For the next few years, we continue to see the two of them. Dixie develops into a loving, appropriate mother. She continues to go to school because day care is provided through school.

We watch little Matthew grow up to be a nice kid. He is an active five-year-old the last time I see him. Dixie is with a new boyfriend by then. She is 20. Her new boyfriend is good to Matthew, but he puts pressure on her to have a child by him. She is resisting. She has asthma and overuses her inhaler like she always does. But she has come through that perilous time: the new mother, a child herself, with a minimal support system.

> **Medical background:** Popular culture supposes that maternal love for a newborn is the result of powerful hormones that kick in after the birth.

The hormonal story is a bit more complicated.

During pregnancy, hormones levels change. The level of estrogen that a woman produces increases a thousandfold. She is a regular factory of estrogen intoxication.

The other hormone that is produced during pregnancy and in the postpartum period is oxytocin. It is released during labor. It is the **Motherhood can be a perilous journey.** same thing as "Pitocin." This is the dread "Pit drip" given to women in labor who are failing to progress. If the cervix is failing to dilate or if the contractions are not strong enough, then the doctor sets up a Pitocin drip. This triggers a dramatic increase in the strength of contractions. The pain becomes worse. It is a good idea to get pain meds on board before the doctor turns on a Pit drip.

Besides promoting childbirth, oxytocin continues to be released postpartum. Its job is now to promote breastfeeding. Many medical experts believe that it facilitates bonding of the mother to the newborn as well. While it may facilitate bonding with the baby, it is not a fail-safe. The bonding is much more complicated, as any mother can tell you.

what this case taught me:

The larger society pretends that every mother immediately falls in love with her newborn. This is not true. Motherhood can be a perilous journey. The transition from the physical birth of a child to loving that child is fraught with pitfalls. Not only does it involve a hormonal pulse of oxytocin, but it also requires enough peace of mind and physical and emotional support to make the transition.

I saw one other fifteen-year-old mother with a small baby. This was during residency, during my training at the Big City Hospital. She had brought the baby to the hospital because it was not gaining weight. We did the usual tests. There was no underlying disease. The baby was simply not getting enough to eat. Usually, the baby cries when she is hungry. Usually, the mother responds by feeding her. This 15 year old was not responding to the baby's signals. The baby stopped crying, but the baby was still hungry.

We should not have sent them home.

We reassured the young mother that the baby was healthy but needed to be fed every so many hours. She went home with her baby. We should not have sent them home. We did not know them or their situation well enough. We were in the big city. The mother and baby lived in a small town in eastern Kentucky. The baby died one month later from failure to thrive. The bond between mother and baby was just not there. The fifteen-year-old herself had no mother. Her mother had died three years earlier.

Another patient I see early on in my tenure as a physician in town is a young woman with a sad story. As a doctor, people tell you stories. Many of these stories are heartbreaking, and I didn't know how to deal with them at first.

the heart develops a callus
I give her a hug and weep with her.

A young woman whose child had died in a fire tells me her story. This had happened two years in the past, but she is telling the story like it just happened.

My house caught fire. I was trying to escape, climbing through a window. I had my two-year-old little girl by the hand and was trying to get her out the window with me. The child let go of my hand. I couldn't find her in the smoke. Finally, I jumped from the window. My child died.

The patient is in her early twenties. She is on medicines for depression. She is poor and overweight, and her clothes are from Goodwill. She cries as she recites this story.

I give her a hug and weep with her. At first, I find it unbearable to hear this story. As a mother of three children, the thought of losing a child is beyond comprehension.

The second time I see this patient, she tells me the story again. This time, it does not hurt so much. She will tell this story every time she sees me. By the third time, my heart has formed a callus. It hurts less and less with each telling.

Do the patients know their stories affect doctors so much?

what this taught me:

I always hear terrible things. This patient teaches me that I can deal with the pain. That the heartache will lessen with time because a callus will form—and life goes on from there.

Local Color

a suburban yankee in the rural south

I settled into my practice. I have been here some years. I still have some things to learn, though.

I learn where you get goat milk if there is no Whole Foods nearby. I see a baby in the clinic who cannot tolerate ordinary formula. The family tries soy formula and then more exotic formulas. They finally try goat milk. They tell me it works well. The baby is thriving.

I ask them where they buy goat milk. I don't see any on the shelves of the local grocery stores. They reply, with some amusement: "from a goat." They explain, for the edification of my city-bred self, that they keep a goat in the front yard and would go out and milk her. I honestly had not thought of that scenario.

Another chapter in my rural education happens in the spring. As I drive into town, I drive past farms with horses in the pastures. Sometimes I pass other farms with donkeys or with sheep. One farm has miniature horses called Shetlands. One day *en route* to work,, I notice miniature sheep. I mention this to the staff. They explain that the dwarf sheep are actually lambs. It is springtime, also known as "lambing season." Again, the staff enjoys endless amusement at my city-bred ignorance.

I also learn a lot about harvesting tobacco. Did you know you can get tobacco poisoning and nearly die from an overdose of nicotine? Neither did I. Not until a young farm worker brought in from Mexico for the tobacco harvest presented in the ER.

He has dangerously high blood pressure and is sweating uncontrollably. He feels dizzy and can't sit up in the ER. He is harvesting tobacco leaves from the field, so the leaves can be hung up to dry in the barn. He is working in short sleeves. Apparently, skin to skin contact with fresh tobacco leaves cause tobacco poisoning.

Fortunately, the owner of the tobacco farm knows all about this medical entity and tells me what is wrong with the worker. After his ER visit, I believe the young man understands to keep covered up, no matter how hot the day is.

CHAPTER THREE

circuitous path to medical school

I wasn't sure why I was there,
so I left school after two years and went to work.

ow did I get from a childhood in the suburbs of Cleveland, Ohio, to serving as a doctor in a small town in Kentucky? I would sometimes ask myself this question. The journey was circuitous and involved college in Boston and travels across the country. Then a marriage and raising a child—and, of course, medical school.

Included: Memories of the sea changes in American society of the 1970s—among them, the second wave of feminism and the opening of professional schools—including medical schools—to women.

college, the first time

My father was a factory worker. In the 1950s and 1960s, many dads worked in Cleveland factories. The money was enough to house and clothe a family of five, although there was nothing left over for luxuries like new furniture or summer camps. However, the local schools were good. The neighborhood consisted of modest two-story houses, each with a tiny patch of grass in the backyard.

I was a shy kid. I sought solace in books. I read lots and lots of books. My vocabulary was based on Dickens. There were many words I knew. I did not know how to pronounce them, though. I had never heard them spoken.

This changed when I went to college the first time. I got a scholarship to go to Brandeis University, a prestigious college near Boston. People used these fancy words at this upscale school. I was surprised to discover that "charisma" has a hard "k" sound when pronounced correctly, and that "Nietzsche" has only two syllables. Who knew?

I also learned other things during that first foray into college. Mostly, I remember the turmoil on campus during the midst of the Vietnam War. Protests were everywhere.

The early 1970s were a confusing time to be in college. I wasn't sure why I was there, so I left school after two years and went to work. I earned enough money for travel.

My extensive reading had given me role models of young people who traveled the globe. Back in the day, many books were written about young men finding themselves. The literary role models were all male, but I could be creative and transpose them into female. The dearth of women's stories changed with the Women's Movement.

college, the second time,
along with motherhood
and the women's movement

I got married and had a baby.

During the pregnancy, I started going to classes again at a local university. I found comfort in taking a math course. I got through nightly bouts of heartburn—a common complaint of late pregnancy —by solving math problems.

I found the rigorous logic of math a welcome relief from the emotional ups and downs of my daily life. I was quite pregnant when I became inspired to take classes in biology. I was intrigued by the wonders of embryology; basically, the science of how a baby grows inside the womb. It seemed like a miracle to me.

Then I met a young woman who was training to be a physician assistant. Every time I saw her, she as carrying big, heavy books. To me, these books looked inviting. After all, I was good at book learning. I started taking pre-med classes that enabled me to apply for the same program.

When I returned to class with baby in arms, the class applauded.

I enjoyed the logic and beauty of chemistry, as well as the elegance of biology. I did not care much for physics, but somehow, I managed.

October arrived and so did my baby. I missed one week of classes. When I returned to class with baby in arms, the class applauded. A memorable moment, but perhaps also a hallmark of my naïveté. I did not know much of anything about raising a child. It's usually not a good idea to bring a baby to chemistry class.

Eventually, I got my child care and part-time classes squared away and continued in school. By the time I got my Bachelor of Arts degree in biology, the physician assistant program had disappeared. Instead, I began to think about going to medical school. Many of my fellow students in these various pre-med courses were aspiring doctors. I figured if they could qualify, so could I!

The Women's Movement had started. This was the second wave of the Women's Movement. The first one was in the 1920s and led to women gaining the vote. This one was heralded by the publication of *Ms. Magazine* with Gloria Steinem as editor. Steinem told us women to seek careers, to be ambitious like the men around us. She declared that the having and raising of children was an inadequate challenge for us, the enlightened ones.

This was an exciting time for me. *Ms. Magazine* explored how deeply sexism pervaded our daily lives. Even the very word "sexism" was a revelation to me. I was twenty-three years old when I first read what became the women's manifesto for many. *Ms. Magazine* and its insights struck me like thunder. This concept of sexism explained why, as a bright female student, I felt so perplexed when I went to college the first time. The college offered the directive to become a social worker, teacher, or nurse for female students. I faced a lack of role models of women in other professions.

So, while this struck me like a bombshell, it was also confounding. I was quite pregnant when I first read Gloria Steinem's op-ed pieces. I was discovering, after all, that the work of pregnancy was nothing to scoff at. I found pregnancy a metaphysical wonder, with the birth of a miniature human at the end of a painful labor. I found mother-hood a pull on my heartstrings.

The feelings of love I had for the baby were unexpected. The fear I had for her when she ran a fever of 103 and was hospitalized for a presumptive meningitis at age two months was more intense than anything I'd experienced before. The night in the ER and then waiting for the following dawn was terrifying, and the relief I felt in the morning when her fever broke. She was alert and even smiling again. I would never underestimate the work of mothering after this experience. It is the most challenging and most engaging work there is.

Gee, I could become a doctor.

Although it is true that conversations with a small child can be mentally draining, I found a rhythm I enjoyed: part-time school, part-time motherhood. My little girl grew up and so did I.

In the interim, the Bakke decision had been implemented. Up to this point, medical students were 95% male. It had been the prerogative of the medical schools to accept whomever they pleased, and they were pleased to accept young white men in their early 20s, ideally, the sons of physicians. The Bakke case was brought by a white male who was in his 30s who had been denied admission based on age, but it opened the floodgates for women and minorities as well. The medical schools were told they could no longer discriminate based on age, race, or gender in terms of admissions.

Suddenly, the option of medical school loomed in the distance. Other friends were going to law school. This was the class of 1973, which was the very first female law school class admitted after the Bakke decision. The medical schools were likewise under pressure to admit women. What had been a silly, nebulous thought before—"Gee, I could become a doctor"—suddenly became a real possibility.

It took some time before that possibility became reality. There were personal and financial challenges *en route*. I divorced my first husband, and I struggled as a single mom for some years. Eventually, I remarried.

One challenge was uprooting the family and moving to Kentucky for my second husband's job. But I eventually arrived, sitting in the lecture hall in medical school, along with one hundred other eager medical students.

medical school days

When I started medical school, it was a male fraternity with a spattering of women in the class. I was thrilled to be joining this social club, although the pretty nurses in the trauma ICU mostly ignored us female medical students and lavished their attention on the handsome male medical students. Although the lectures were mostly tailored to an audience of young men, who hushed and became reverential when anything to do with male body parts was being taught. Nonetheless, it proved an entrée to the rich tradition of doctoring.

Thankfully, I met a woman during the first week of medical school who became my friend.

meeting lauren

Lauren stood out among the other members of the medical school class. She looked different. I first thought she was Mennonite or Amish. Two long brown braids wound down her back, framing a classic face from the British Isles with pleasant cheekbones and even features. She possessed a very dry way of talking. She dressed in simple cotton clothes, further enhancing the feeling of a religious aesthete. She was also older, in her mid-thirties. Most medical students' ages ranged from 22 to 30 years old.

The two of us were close in age. I approached her as we spilled out of lecture into the hallway for a ten-minute break. I said something like "I could not understand a word that that lecturer said, what with his accent … ." She looked at me askance, gave a cursory acknowledgement of my existence, and that was the end of that attempt at conversation.

The next day, she was slightly more talkative. Eventually, we became friends, and she became my study partner. She took wonderful lecture notes that were both legible and coherent. Her notes served as a valuable commodity if ever I missed a lecture.

She was terribly bright—but never warm, fuzzy, or sociable. Our interactions, however, over the years, evolved into a pattern. I would come to her house for coffee. She and her seven cats would greet me. She was the first person I told—other than my husband—that I was pregnant, which was an unexpected treat. In the preceding seven years of trying, I had been unable to get pregnant. By the time I started medical school, I had basically given up on the idea of having more children.

"Did you mean to get pregnant?" she asked, in her typically dry, unembellished style.

"No, but I am thrilled in any event," I answered.

The following summer, she welcomed both me and the new baby to her home. She did not judge; she just accepted. For this, I was eternally grateful.

We helped each other navigate the four years of medical school, and the internship and residency that followed. Her medical advice helped me navigate some of the trickier cases I saw during my time as a physician. She was my good friend, and I was blessed that she came into my life.

CHAPTER FOUR

training in the big city hospital—the NICU

Surely the name tags would trigger a sense of doom in anyone.

The hospital where I trained had a Neonatal Intensive Care Unit—known by all in the hospital as the NICU. This NICU would take premature babies and sick newborns from all over the state. Some of these preemies did well, but some did not fare well. A number of these infants would be left with vision problems or developmental delays. I felt bad for the young mothers whose babies had gone through a rough road in the NICU. The young mothers had no idea what to expect.

But I knew. I had already raised a child and I knew that raising a normal, healthy child is challenge enough.

As I mentioned, I became pregnant during medical school. I spent a fair amount of time in training in the NICU as my pregnancy progressed.

I also became superstitious during the pregnancy. I could not look at African masks that decorated the walls of the local upscale café. They looked malevolent. I could not pass the NICU without saying a prayer: *No, God forbid, don't let the NICU get this baby!* Then, when I made it past 28 weeks, the age at which most babies survive on their own, I would say out loud, "Aha! The NICU is NOT getting this one!"

the power of names

Due to the difficulties surrounding their births, there are often twins in the NICU. Twins are difficult to carry and are often born premature, as early as 25 or 26 weeks. They are tiny at this stage; no more than two pounds. They need supplemental oxygen because their little lungs are not mature enough to breathe on their own.

Unfortunately, the premature babies often die, despite the best efforts of the skilled nurses and the highly-trained physicians.

As a newbie trainee in the unit, I grow used to hearing the endless *beeps* of ventilators and alarms going off at all hours. I notice how fragile these preemies are. When I see two new admissions, in adjoining bassinets, who are named "Angelwing A" and "Angelwing B," I get a sense of foreboding. Surely the name tags would trigger a sense of doom in anyone. These are NOT good names to have, not in the middle of the high-pressure NICU.

On the other hand, two other babies, a bit larger than the Angelwing boys, are in neighboring bassinets. Their names are "Wigglesbottom A and B." Now that's an excellent surname, which suggests an active constitution, and bodes well for life after the NICU.

In fact, the Angelwing twins die within one week. The Wigglesbottom twins thrive and are discharged home within one month after gaining the requisite weight. I'm sure that I even met the twins twenty years later when they were all grown up. The last name surely can't be that common.

achondroplasia

When I have a few minutes free while covering the NICU, I look at the new admissions, peeking into bassinets on the less intensive side of the NICU. I find a healthy-size baby, a good-looking boy who seems to be full-term. That makes him exceptional in the NICU, where most baby are preemies. He is kicking and active. He looks mighty healthy. I notice that his arms and legs are shorter than normal. An idle thought drifts into my mind: *This kid might have achondroplasia.*

Achondroplasia is the most common dwarfism condition. Famous actors on TV display achondroplasia: a handsome head, body with adult height of less than four feet, with a short torso, arms, and legs. While the thought floats in my sleep-deprived brain for a second, I notice that a grandmotherly-looking lady has just entered the NICU and is heading my way. I notice she is a dwarf as well, no taller than four feet. My powers of deduction are finely tuned; I deduce that this is the baby's grandmother. This coincidence—both baby and grandmother with achondroplasia—pretty much validates the diagnosis of an inherited disorder.

A few minutes later, the mother herself joins the family group. She had just delivered by C-section, so her gait is a bit hampered. Her height matches the grandmother. Mothers with achondroplasia used to die in childbirth; their pelvis is too small to allow birth of a baby. Now that C-sections are so readily available, this little vignette at the baby's bassinet is more common: three generations with achondroplasia. The disease is a perfect demonstration of autosomal dominant inheritance, or a gene passed down from parent to child.

the conjoined twins

I was working the late-night shift. I would start at 5 p.m. and work, often nonstop, until 7 a.m. the next morning. Part of my job was to visit all the babies in their individual bassinets, and check intake and output. How much had they eaten that day, how much they had peed, and had passed any stool. This was definitely not the most exciting part of my training.

So here I am at around 11 p.m. I steadily perform rounds on ten or so preemies. As I said before, most babies in the NICU are preemies. A fair number are twin or even triplet births. Besides needing supplemental oxygen for their immature lungs, they often needed nutrition via a feeding tube. This is a tube that went directly into their little stomachs.

I come to bassinet #11. I dutifully record the data on intake and output from Twin A. I then look for Twin B. I did not have to look far; Twin B is in the same bassinet! It turns out they are conjoined twins, attached across the sternum. There are two separate heads and two bodies, but unfortunately they share only one kidney and other parts of the pelvis are conjoined. The second twin is smaller than the first, with a misshapen head.

Somehow, I have not processed that conjoined twins were admitted to the NICU.

The conjoined twins are headed to surgery and the surgeons will attempt to separate them. The strain on their shared kidney is excessive. If not separated, they will both die. The surgeons manage to separate them in an intricate procedure. Twin A survives. Twin B does not.

Discussion of conjoined twins: Conjoined twins are rare. And most of the time, they are stillborn, or they die shortly after birth. They are also known as "Siamese twins," after the famous Barnum circus presented Chang and Eng, conjoined twins from Siam, as a circus act in the 1820s. They toured with the circus for years. They both married and even had children, marrying sisters. The connubial act(s) must have been complicated, one speculates. Chang died at age 63. His brother's death followed a few minutes later.

The incidence of viable conjoined twins is perhaps one in every 300,000 births. They were in the NICU because the Big City Hospital had excellent pediatric surgeons on staff. The conjoined twins had been flown in by helicopter from an outlying hospital.

Identical twins arise when a single early embryo splits evenly into two separate embryos. The two embryos then proceed to develop into two separate fetuses.

Conjoined twins arise when identical twin fetuses somehow share tissue during development as represented in my diagram.

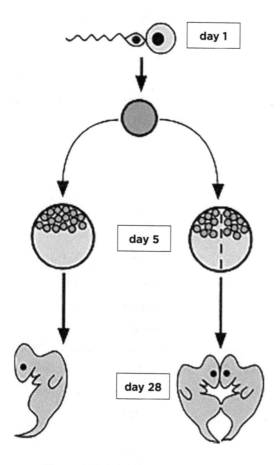

day 1

day 5

day 28

Figure 1. Origin of conjoined twins

Day 1: Fertilization of egg by sperm. By Day 5: The fertilized egg has undergone several rounds of cell division. It has given rise to an 18-cell embryonic mass encased in a protective shell.

In a normal sequence, the 18-cell embryonic mass develops into a single fetus. In the 1/30 occasion of an error—the 18-cell mass divides neatly into two–then identical twins occur. If the 18-cell mass fails to divide neatly into two ... then the two bodies are conjoined.

In the case shown in my diagram, there are two separate spines, as well as two sets of arms and legs. The fusion happens at the level of the abdomen. One of the twins has a weak heart and a less developed brain. This can be termed "a parasitic twin." The fetuses' survival depend on the stronger twin maintaining circulation for both of them. In essence, the weaker twin is *dependent on the larger twin for survival. There was asymmetry from the beginning.*

what this case taught me:

*When it came time to separate the conjoined twins,
the surgeons decided to sacrifice the one that was already
faltering. The child on the right had a smaller head and
appeared less alert. The surgeons gave the one on the left the
intact kidney and pelvis. It was not possible to save
both twins, so a decision needed to be made. That is the
nature of life.*

CHAPTER FIVE

genetic diseases, kentucky gene pool

My fascination for genetic disorders persisted.

A s time moved on, I have completed my training. I am now working in the small town of Dry Lick, running my own practice. I get my feet wet with the mysteries of coon hunting and Mountain Dew. I see a young mother bonding to her baby. I am beginning to know my patients. I am also beginning to see some interesting genetic diseases.

My training was originally in genetics. I worked as a genetic counselor and in research for some years before attending medical school. My fascination for genetic

Cousins marry their cousins, sometimes even first cousins.

disorders persisted. I somehow manage, while in practice, to see several families with exquisitely rare genetic diseases. These diseases are known as "autosomal recessive." They occur in a child only if he or she inherits a gene defect in a double dose: one defective gene from each parent. Keep in mind rare diseases should occur in maybe one out of a million people. I see several such cases in my practice that is in a small community.

Maybe I am seeing more of them because of the isolation between towns in Appalachia. The isolation is so profound that people tended to stay within their own patch of the mountains and to marry other folk who lived nearby. Cousins marry their cousins, sometimes even first cousins. If the married first cousins have children together, the risk for genetic disease is much higher than it would be in an "outbred" population. This is also true for the Amish population in Pennsylvania. They too can have babies born with rare diseases due to intermarriage within the tight-knit community.

The other cause for the appearance of a rare genetic disease is, of course, in the case of incest: a relationship closer than that of cousins.

Below are three patient cases related to genetic diseases, followed by a short discussion of the nature of the Kentucky gene pool and how inbreeding may contribute to the frequency of genetic disease.

a very pretty girl

We do an ultrasound of her bladder.
The bladder appears hugely distended.

Anna Glass is twelve years old. She is a very pretty girl, with blue-green eyes and blonde hair. She is legally blind. Something exotic, her mother tells me, is causing her to slowly lose her vision. She sees an eye specialist.

Mom has brought Anna in to see me. She is worried because Anna was just hospitalized for three days. "This is the third time this year she's been hospitalized," her mom tells me. Every time, it is because she gets a stomach flu and starts throwing up. Anna ends up in the hospital in serious condition, apparently dehydrating quickly. She gets intravenous fluids for three days and recovers quickly.

Mom also mentions that Anna has always urinated often. Even as a toddler, she had to pee frequently. She also drinks a lot of water. Mom said her urine looks like clear water, with hardly any color to it.

I ask Anna to leave a urine sample. The urine does look clear, with no yellow tint to it whatsoever. Further tests confirm that Anna has problems concentrating her urine. No wonder she must drink nonstop. Everything she drinks goes right through her. Her body is unable to hold onto the fluids she takes in by drinking. If she fails to have access to water or if she is throwing up and can't keep down anything, then she dehydrates within a short interval. Her life depends on replenishment of water for her body.

An ultrasound is done of her bladder—hers appears hugely distended.

Anna is drinking 12 liters daily and peeing out 12 liters daily. This is three times the normal liquid amount the body should need.

She goes down the road to see the pediatric kidney specialist. The specialist confirms a kidney disease. Her kidneys are unable to reabsorb the water that her body requires. The specialist says this is something she was born with, and there is no treatment. Anna's kidney damage is progressive, and she will require a kidney transplant soon.

It turns out that she has an exquisitely rare gene defect that accounts not only for the kidney problems, but also for her ongoing vision loss. The defect is autosomal recessive meaning she has to have inherited an abnormal gene from her mom and her dad.

Anna's parents are both from the same small town in Tennessee. They deny being related to each other, although they do admit they both have grandparents with the same last name. Presumably, her parents are second or third cousins to each other, whether they know it or not.

What gene defect can cause damage both to the kidneys and to the retina?

At age sixteen, Anna did go on to receive a kidney transplant. The parents told me that I had saved her life. Few patients say that, so I remember it clearly.

After the transplant, Anna did well. She contacted me via Facebook some ten years later. She had gone to college and was helping raise her fiancé's children. She had been told, in no uncertain terms, not to risk a pregnancy herself. The transplanted kidney would not adequately handle the stress of a pregnancy.

Medical Perspective: This patient had a kidney defect, such that she was unable to produce concentrated urine. The kidneys usually absorb water back into the bloodstream. She was failing to reabsorb the water. Instead, the water continued onward, through her kidneys, into her bladder as urine that resulted in a grossly distended bladder. The urine was so diluted that it was clear in color.

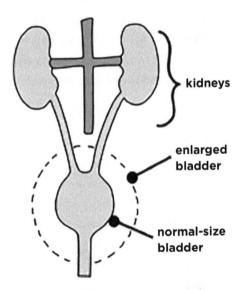

Figure 2. Urinary tract

She also had an eye problem, She was born with defective development of the cells that make up the retina. Her loss of vision is slowly progressive, leading to blindness due to ongoing degeneration of the retina, the light-sensitive layer at the back of the eye.

What underlying defect, what gene defect, can cause damage both to the kidneys and to the retina? This is a bit murky. Normal development of the kidneys and the retina apparently requires activation of a particular gene. In the absence of this gene—and that is what a recessive disorder entails, the complete absence of a gene—the eyes and the kidney fail to develop as they should.

bones turning into stone

The child in front of me obviously has a severe form of the disease for it to manifest in infancy.

The mother is sixteen years old. She is pushing a stroller into clinic. It is a hot day and she has walked about three miles to get to the clinic, telling the staff she got here as fast as she could, after getting out of school at 3 p.m.

My first thought is: *She would have been pretty if she did not look so tired.*

I bend down to admire the baby in the stroller. He is tiny. I am about to say the usual inane things that people say to little babies, "Ooh! Look at you! So big, with those chubby legs of yours!" These words and sentiments die on my lips after one look at his gaunt under-sized face, protruding eyes, and little twigs for legs.

"How old is he?" I ask.

"Four months," she says.

My heart sinks at her answer. I know there is something very wrong with him. He doesn't weigh any more than ten pounds, which is the size of a normal two month old.

Mom and her baby settle into the exam room. I sit down and review his hefty paper chart. The word that grabs my attention is *osteopetrosis*. This word is one of those Greek words that are sprinkled throughout medical books.

Remember, this happened in the days before information could be researched on laptops and Google. Another physician in the clinic provides a translation: *bones turning into stone.*

He is failing to thrive.

It sounds like *osteoporosis*: the thinning of the bones that happens as a person gets older. This is the opposite. It is a disease of bone metabolism that makes the bones too dense. The child in front of me obviously has a severe form of the disease for it to manifest in infancy. My heart sinks; his prognosis is poor. That is a euphemism for "We have absolutely no treatment for this. He will die soon. I am sorry."

The young mother brings him every two weeks for visits to the clinic. He needs medicine to control the levels of calcium in his body. She thinks this will help him get better.

In fact, as it turns out, controlling his calcium or phosphate never does affect the overall course of the disease. As I see him for further visits, it is obvious that he is losing vision and hearing. The nerves running to the eyes or to the ears are being damaged, due to compression in the bony canals through which they run. The opening in the skull, at the base of the brain, is also closing off. It is compressing the brainstem. He is failing to thrive.

The mother keeps bringing him in for his regular visits. There is nothing we can do for him.

Two months later, he dies. He is six months old.

suspicions of his origins

I visit the mother's house on the day of his funeral, to offer my condolences and bring flowers. The house is a modest one, next door to old tobacco warehouses, on a rough side of town. I knock on the door, which is opened by her father, a middle-aged man who is missing a leg and walks with a prosthesis. There is no wife in the house.

Whenever a child is born with a rare autosomal recessive disorder —like osteopetrosis—then the question always arises: "Are the parents related to each other?" The answer is often, "Yes," as first cousins or even closer. How else would the same rare gene be given to a child in a double dose? That would only happen if each parent carried a copy of the mutant gene.

In this case, I never asked the mother who had fathered the baby. The question seemed inopportune at the time. I hope she was safe in her house. In hindsight, I wish we had talked to her about our concerns for her safety.

Medical background: The baby was born with an exquisitely rare disorder, where the cells that promote deposition of bone were uncontrolled. Bone gets laid down by cells called "osteoblasts," and then it gets remodeled by the remodeling team, cells known as "osteoclasts." But the dance between deposition and destruction of bony matrix was no longer operative. The bones became too dense and turned into stone.

Figure 3. Osteoclasts and bone remodeling

From a review of literature a few years ago, the only known treatment for this condition. The cells that control bone maturation, the osteoclasts and osteoblasts, arise from bone marrow. If a patient's bone marrow is destroyed and replaced with normal cells from a donor, then the donor cells will hopefully repopulate the bone marrow, such that further remodeling of the bony matrix is normal, and the bones regain a normal density.

This treatment works in a small percentage of patients. I saw this patient in 1995, when bone marrow transplantation was a new experimental procedure. Twenty-three years later, it is still an experimental procedure for patients with osteopetrosis. Some infants show marginal improvement, and some infants die because of graft failure.

what this case taught me:

1. *The devotion and strength of the young mother. She brings him into clinic, come rain or shine, every week. She believes what we tell her. She does not fight the reality that he is going to die. She accepts it.*

2. *The wisdom of Dr. Lake, the specialist who sees the baby and gives me guidance on how to treat him. She has been in practice for 25 years. Dr. Lake knew about bone marrow transplantation and that there was an experimental program available in Philadelphia.*

3. *She told me NOT to tell the young mother about the dangerous procedure. The young mother had no resources to go to Philadelphia and prepare to stay there for months. Plus, the baby was already in poor condition. The damage was already done; a bone marrow transplant would not reverse it. He had already suffered significant damage to the spinal cord.*

I respected Dr. Lake's decision. There are always risks with any medical treatment. The trick is to calculate the possible benefit and decide whether it is worth the risks. Sometimes the calculated answer is: "No, the treatment is too dangerous, too painful, the benefits too uncertain."

I see this calculation at play years later with a patient who was going through multiple rounds of chemo for a lymphoma that was becoming resistant to treatment. He chooses to stop any further treatment. I respect this decision as well, to call it quits. The side effects of chemotherapy are burdensome and painful, and he is getting no better. There is a limit to what doctors can fix.

the blue people

It ain't no big deal. Everybody in the family is blue.
His grandma is blue. His other auntie is blue.

A doctor in Lexington, Kentucky, told me the following story:

"I had been working in the NICU in 1975 when a blue baby was brought in by ambulance. He was one day old. He had been brought in from a small community in eastern Kentucky. The doctor who delivered him saw his color stayed blue and he panicked. He was convinced the baby had a bad heart defect and wanted a pediatric cardiologist to take over his care."

It is understood that a newborn baby is normally pink in color, at least those of the Caucasian persuasion. A blue baby usually means the heart is not working well. The heart is failing as a pump. Oxygen-rich blood from the lungs is NOT being pumped to the extremities. Oxygen-poor blood is blue in color, like the color of the veins.

The doctor continues her story. "We paged the pediatric cardiologist to come to the NICU ASAP. Heck, it was an overhead page,

'Dr. O'Malley, to the NICU STAT!' It takes maybe five minutes for him to get down here. Meanwhile, it turns out the aunt had come in with the newborn. She had tagged along in the ambulance. The aunt taps me on the shoulder and says: 'I don't see why they had to rush little Matthew here like that! There ain't nothing wrong with him!'

The doctor-storyteller says she turned to the aunt in disbelief. She said to her, "I am so sorry, the baby is blue. I am afraid he has a heart problem. He may need surgery. We are waiting for the cardiologist to examine him … he will be here in a minute." The aunt says, "Why would he need any kind of heart surgery?" The doctor answered, "Because he is blue! That means he has a heart problem!"

Now, doctors in the NICU are familiar with the patient population from eastern Kentucky. Such patients are often uneducated. No doubt the aunt did not appreciate the severity of the situation.

The aunt replies, with some indignation: "It ain't no big deal. Everybody in the family is blue. His grandma is blue. His other auntie is blue." The informant did not appear to be worried. She was simply confused as to why everyone was panicking over the color of her newborn nephew.

Indeed, when the cardiologist arrived and did all the tests that cardiologists do—including an echocardiogram to analyze the structure of the heart—he declared the heart perfectly normal. He did not know why the child was blue.

The NICU doctor told the cardiologist what the aunt had said. That everyone in the family was blue. This was quite a remarkable statement. However, it turned out that the aunt was speaking the truth.

More blue babies continued to be born.

Upon further investigation—and the taking of a family history—it turned out that this child was descended from the "Blue Fugates of Kentucky," who were famous (or infamous) for a genetic defect that caused them to have entirely blue skin. This had been reported by a hematologist in the 1960s.

The family came from Troublesome Creek. This was one of the hollows deep in the mountains. A gentleman named Fugate had settled there in 1820. He married a young woman by the name of Smith; whether she was a niece of his is unclear. They had ten children and four of them were blue. The family continued to live in Troublesome Creek, as did their grandchildren.

Cousins married cousins. More blue babies continued to be born, up until roads were built into the mountains and folk could more easily travel outside their hometown and find spouses who were unrelated to them. This increased mobility started happening in the 1930s and 1940s. Fewer blue babies were born thereafter.

The researcher who first studied the family concluded that the blue color was due to a double dose of a recessive gene, that each parent must have carried at least one copy of the gene defect and passed it along in double dose to a child. The gene defect involved a failure of the red blood cells to pick up oxygen as briskly as they were supposed to. With decreased oxygen content, the blood takes on a bluish hue that is reflected in the color of the skin.

Strangely enough, it caused no serious problems for those affected. There were enough normally functioning red blood cells that the individuals were able to carry on without any adverse effects. Their problem was solely a cosmetic one: they were bluish in color.

In fact, the doctor-researcher was able to give them a blue dye to take by mouth. It eliminated the blue color temporarily. They voided the blue pigment into their urine. Their skin pinked up nicely.

Apparently, the blue color had been a source of shame for the family. The neighbors in Troublesome Creek had never thought highly of the blue people. They were treated like an anomaly. Thus, these people were delighted to be able to opt for a pink complexion instead, as long as they took daily doses of the blue dye.

This disorder is exquisitely rare. The only other family known to have this disorder is an Eskimo kindred in the depths of Alaska. Again, this occurred because of geographic isolation and a degree of inbreeding.

By the way, the baby boy in the NICU did fine. He was sent home within a couple of days, back to his family in eastern Kentucky.

appalachian history and the kentucky gene pool

If you are born in a given town, you will probably find a mate nearby and probably spend your life in the area.

Indians have always had a presence in the southern part of the country. For thousands of years, before Europeans arrived in North America, they had hunted for game in the forests.

White settlers first came to Appalachia in the early 1700s. Scotch-Irish colonists fled the Quaker-controlled East Coast and headed west to the wilderness. More settlers from the British Isles—mostly English from a county bordering on Scotland—followed suit. After Daniel Boone found the Cumberland Pass, it encouraged another influx of settlement in the 1770s.

There is some speculation that immigration was incentivized by the War of Independence. Those who chose not to fight in the War of Independence voted with their feet and left behind the thirteen colonies on the East Coast.

These settlers remained sequestered in the hills and valleys of Appalachia. When asked about their ancestry, they always answer: "Why, we are American!" They do not understand that their grandparents or great-grandparents or great-great-grandparents came from

A lot of folk told me they were "kin to themselves."

somewhere else. They have always lived in these mountains, as far as they know.

Scottish-Irish-English background shows up in a few ways, all these years later. The Southern accent is related to an old dialect of

English that was spoken on the border with Scotland. Their genetics all follow suit. They have a certain look: fair skin, brown hair, and blue or green eyes. They settled in the "hollows," the valleys that run between the mountains.

In those hollows, towns are separated by mountain ranges. One does not easily travel from one place to another. If you are born in a given town, you will probably find a mate nearby and probably spend your life in the area.

A lot of folk told me they were "kin to themselves." It was only in the last fifty years or so, when roads were put in, that folk started mixing it up some. If you can drive down the road, out of your area to a new town, you are more likely to meet and marry someone who is NOT a cousin.

This tendency to marry kin was true for all who lived in the hills of Appalachia. The gene pool was largely Caucasian and Anglo-Saxon.

There were exceptions, of course. There were pockets of folk deep in the mountains whose great-grandparents had been Italian immigrants, mixed in with Cherokee and African-American as well. The Italians came to the mountains as miners in the early 1800s. They were called "Melungeons." I met one such family. They had black curly hair and olive-toned skin. They looked totally different from everyone else in town.

There was also the family with the surname of Boone. They had straight black hair and dark eyes. They were clearly part Cherokee. They told me they were descended from Daniel Boone's brother. The irony was that Daniel Boone had fought the Cherokee and other Indian tribes during the War of Independence. His son had been killed by the Indians during the last battle of the War for Independence. Apparently, the family had made peace with the Cherokee thereafter.

The other irony is that the last battle of the War for Independence occurred two months after the War officially ended. The news of the peace treaty had failed to travel inland, so, in 1775, the Indians—who were allies of the British—and the settlers in Kentucky still fought a battle to the death two months after the war ended. It was Mark Twain who said: "I want to live in Kentucky when the world ends. It always takes a while for any news to reach them."

There had always been a small community of African-Americans who lived in town. Descendants of slaves, they had a separate church and a separate graveyard.

Interestingly, the Underground Railroad ran through this section of Kentucky. Some white people had set aside secret rooms in their basements to house runaway slaves. Slaves escaped from the deep south, trying to cross the Ohio River to freedom. The book *Uncle Tom's Cabin* described someone trying to make such a crossing.

CHAPTER SIX

our froggy heritage

The connection with lizards and frogs
shows up in unusual ways.

Many people who live in Kentucky are southern Baptists or evangelicals. They do not believe in evolution. They believe that God created the world in six days, and that apes and humans are not related to each other. The Creation Museum in Petersburg, Kentucky, features dioramas illustrating the coexistence of mankind and dinosaurs.

In contrast, I came from the world of biochemistry and genetics. I was fascinated by the discoveries that confirmed the unity of life. That microbes share genes with starfish; that the genetic code that encodes "make a limb" is identical, whether it's being activated in a frog or a human. I took pleasure in researching the kinship of life across phyla and genera.

The connection with lizards and frogs shows up in unusual ways, even in a small medical clinic. The following two cases illustrate this.

the baby has thumbs!
It takes a few seconds to process what she is telling me.

I meet Carol in the clinic. She is 34 years old, a bit overweight, sensibly but not fashionably dressed. She comes in about a cough that is easily treated. I notice she has some abnormalities of her arms. Her forearms are too short. Each of her hands is also missing a thumb.

She tells me she has Holt-Oram syndrome. This is a birth defect that leads to underdevelopment of the bones in her arms. Her mother has the same thing, as does a sister. This is clearly an autosomal dominant disorder: a gene defect passed on from parent to child.

One would think that the absence of thumbs would be a major hindrance. However, Carol has done remarkably well despite this impediment. She has raised a 14-year-old boy, largely by herself. He was in junior high and doing fine, according to his proud mother.

Jump ahead two years. Carol is pregnant! She has a boyfriend. Carol is thrilled with the pregnancy and is looking forward to raising another baby. Her 16-year-old son is less than thrilled at the prospect of a new baby, but what teenage boy would feel otherwise?

Carol is now four months pregnant. On her next visit to the clinic, she tells me the results of her recent ultrasound. Her first descriptor: "She has thumbs!" It takes a few seconds to process what she is telling me. One, the baby is a girl. Two, she has thumbs. Most parents would not highlight the thumb issue so prominently. Carol is thrilled that her soon-to-be daughter would be born normal, at least in the thumbs department.

The baby is born and is lovely, happy, and healthy. She grows up quickly and she has the manual dexterity to help her mother when needed.

Medical Background: Holt-Oram syndrome is named after the physicians who first described the condition. "Sonic hedgehog" is the name of the gene that triggers development of the limb buds in humans in utero, at about six weeks gestation. The same gene triggers limb development in all our evolutionary antecedents, including the legs of lizards all the way through the mammalian line, leading to the great apes and us.

My grandson tells me "Sonic the Hedgehog" is also the name of a video game. Who knew?

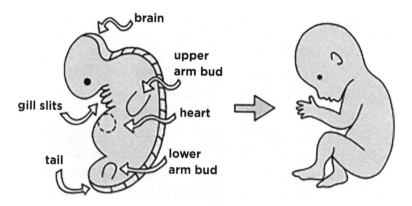

**Figure 4. Development of human embryo:
From 4-weeks to 8-weeks of age.**

Once the limb buds appear, then further genes fine-tune additional development. The upper limb buds turn into arms and hands. The lower limb buds turn into legs and feet. A mutation in one of these downstream genes causes Holt-Oram syndrome. The signal for normal development of bones in the arms and hands goes awry. In my story, the baby is born with foreshortened arms and with missing thumbs.

All this development starts with the signal for "make a limb" in the early embryo.

the reptilian brain

Circuits in the cerebellum are similar across all classes of vertebrates, including fish, reptiles, birds, and mammals.

Cindy Keel is a 52 year old social worker at the local hospital. She is complaining of increasing weakness and numbness in both arms and increasing problems with balance. She starts using a cane because she keeps falling.

I send her to the neurologist nearby, who takes her complaints seriously. Numbness in both arms and loss of balance are alarming. Cindy gets an MRI to rule out impingement of the nerves of the neck. The MRI confirms that she has compression of the base of the brain and of the nerves that supply sensation to the arms.

The formal diagnosis is "Arnold-Chiari syndrome." The base of the skull is malformed. It is allowing a basal structure of the brain—the cerebellum—to herniate downward, into the spinal canal.

On a follow-up visit, some months later, Cindy is having increasing problems with loss of coordination and poor balance. She needs a motorized wheelchair to navigate the hospital corridors. The decision is made to go to surgery. The neurosurgeon removes a square inch or so of skull at the nape of the neck. The allows the cerebellum more breathing room. It is less compressed.

I see Cindy in the clinic after surgery. She shows me the surgical scar, over the back of her neck. She does not regain her balance, although she seems to have stabilized. She is finding it increasingly difficult to continue work. She decides to take disability and an early retirement. She stays busy at home now..

The cerebellum, part of the reptilian brain
The cerebellum is the "little brain" tucked behind the brain stem, underneath the more elegant cerebral lobes.

We higher vertebrates credit our cerebral hemisphere with our much-vaunted higher functions: dreaming, thinking, impulse control, and intelligence. The cerebellum gets scant attention. It controls the lesser, albeit essential, functions: balance and motor control.

However, the cerebellum does deserve more respect. Its composition is unique. "Purkinje cells" with extensive branches communicate with other neurons in a tightly organized, almost computerlike system.

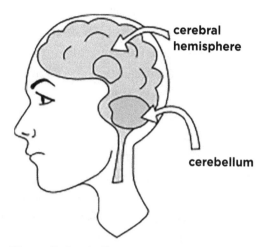

cerebral hemisphere

cerebellum

Figure 5. Cerebellum and cerebral hemispheres

Information from the higher brain gets processed in the cerebellum, with the result being precisely controlled balance, and fine and gross movements.

Damage to the cerebellum causes motor symptoms, such as an abnormal gait and difficulty with balance, which is what this patient had.

Comparative anatomy and evolution.
Circuits in the cerebellum are similar across all classes of vertebrates, including fish, reptiles, birds, and mammals. There is even a cerebellar type structure in the brains of octopuses.

The cerebellum in mammals is larger and more convoluted than those of the lower vertebrates. As you ascend one step higher on the evolutionary ladder, to the level of great apes and humans, there exists a further level of complexity. The cerebellum gets larger. Of course, the cerebral hemispheres have enlarged

Its increased size in humans may have contributed to our unique combination of intelligence and adaptability.

as well. But the relative size of the cerebellum shows more of an increase, compared to the increased size of the cerebrum.

Until recently, the cerebellum was thought to be a relic of the reptile brain. The cerebellum was deemed essential for motor control and not much else. Recent studies using functional MRIs have shown that the cerebellum has interconnections with the higher brain areas and may well be involved in language, attention, and mental imagery. Its increased size in humans may have contributed to our unique combination of intelligence and adaptability.

The pathology in this patient vignette apparently involved only circuitry required for balance and gait. I did not see any other mental status changes in her clinical presentation. Perhaps circuitry for these higher functions are located somewhere other than the lowermost peduncle of the cerebellum, that nubbin of brain that was traumatized in the base of the skull.

CHAPTER SEVEN

cancer and the new genetics

This may go down in history as the Age of Genetics, given how much we have learned in just the space of my lifetime.

Cancers have been described for millennia as masses that grow quickly and extend outward into surrounding tissue, with crablike claws. Ancient people named these deadly growths "the crab." In Latin, the name for "crab" is "cancer." That is why the "sign of the crab" is, in fact, used colloquially to refer to cancer.

The following two stories are about the various manifestations of cancer. The sign of the crab can be obvious. It can be subtle. Cancer is the great pretender. It can present in a myriad of ways and is sometimes difficult to diagnose.

These two patient vignettes are followed by a story about working in the Cancer Center while in training; and then a discussion on cancer genetics and how much has been learned in the last twenty years.

self-diagnosis gone awry

*The attempt to self-diagnose is not uncommon
among physicians and people with medical training.*

I meet Melanie Prather while working alongside her in the Emergency Room. She is a physician assistant, in her mid-forties. An attractive woman, slender and well-dressed; perhaps a bit hyperactive, always moving and speaking fast.

She tells me she went to medical school at age 23 but decided to leave after two years, to get married and to start a family. She has two kids in their twenties. She went back to school at some point, to get her physician assistant degree.

Her son has autism and still lives at home. She tells me he is significantly impaired; she and her husband are looking for an adult care home for him.

One time, as we are chatting, Melanie mentions that she has a disease caused "scleroderma." This is a rather uncommon autoimmune disorder which causes thickening of skin and muscles. She decided on her own that she has scleroderma because she has trouble swallowing. Food gets caught in the esophagus.

She also thinks it is scleroderma which is causing a progressive scarring of her left breast.

She does not have a regular doctor.

I tell her she needs to see a breast specialist, to have a mammogram. She defers. Soon thereafter, a cough develops with shortness of breath. Finally, she goes to the ER herself. A chest X ray shows fluid in her lungs. Fluid in the chest can be a sign of cancer, and it turns out that not only does she have breast cancer, but it has spread to her lungs.

The attempt to self-diagnose is not uncommon among physicians and people with medical training. It is unfortunate. Melanie is distracted by responsibilities as a mother and is high strung. These facts create a perfect storm which led her to rationalize the physical symptoms she had been experiencing for years.

what this case taught me:

Physicians are terrible at diagnosing themselves. They can overthink things, find obscure diagnoses, or delay getting treatment. They can be in denial when it's something serious.

an elusive diagnosis

What do the low red blood cells have to do with her asthma?

Belle Watson is a 70-year-old lady. She has visited the clinic twice before with asthma flare-ups both times, typically with a complaint of, "I'm wheezing; I am short of breath. It's my asthma acting up." The last two times I saw her, I sent her home with the classic combination of meds for asthma flares: home oxygen, steroids, increased nebulizer treatments, and antibiotics. Both times, Belle got better.

Today, her complaint is different. She is weak. She also has shortness of breath. She has been getting worse over the last month. Her oxygen levels are again relatively low, less than 90%, now at 83%. She is unsteady on her feet. Lung sounds are not all that remarkable. I do not hear the tight wheezes she had before, the hallmark of asthma.

Why she is so short of breath remains a mystery. Asthma is no longer a likely culprit. She reluctantly agrees to go to the nearby hospital for labs and a chest X-ray.

The lab calls me in a panic: levels of red blood cells are dangerously low. Her daughter is with her. We convince Belle to go to the "fancy" hospital down the road because she needs a blood transfusion immediately. What do the low red blood cells have to do with her asthma? This is a mystery, at least to me.

Belle makes it to the Big City Hospital uneventfully. The doctors there are also puzzled by her profound anemia. A blood transfusion is initiated. After several hours, and with direct questioning, Belle finally admits she has been having vaginal bleeding for the last three years.

Belle was trying to ignore the bleeding, to pretend it wasn't happening.

The CT scan shows uterine cancer with metastatic disease. The weakness and shortness of breath were unrelated to the long history of asthma. Profuse uterine bleeding and severe anemia were causing the low oxygen levels in this instance.

The patient knew she had uterine cancer. Belle was trying to ignore the bleeding, to pretend it wasn't happening. Human nature sometimes leads people to believe if you don't talk about it, it's not real.

what this case taught me:

Doctors can't always figure it out. Simple deduction sometimes fails. Occam's razor fails. The simplest explanation for her shortness of breath would have been an asthma exacerbation, but not so, in this case. Her shortness of breath had to do with profound anemia due to blood loss, which itself was due to vaginal bleeding and uterine cancer. The doctors had to travel a circuitous path to a diagnosis.

the cancer center

Most patients in the Cancer Unit died—
despite the beautifully appointed rooms.

My introduction to treating cancer had been years before, while in training. I had spent time in the newly built, state-of-the-art Cancer Center. The adult inpatient unit had been a lovely facility. There were lots of windows and spacious patient rooms with comfortable furniture.

The patients who came to this Center were sick. They had cancers that were beyond the ability of regular doctors to treat. Cancer specialists in their home communities had already subjected them to the usual round of chemotherapies and of radiation. The patients only came to this specialty Center because they were not getting better. It was the place of last resort.

They would be enrolled in experimental trials. They would be given a new iteration of a chemotherapy agent and see how they did. And what we meant by experimental medicines back in the day were strong poisons. The medicines were designed to kill rapidly dividing cells.

Ideally, the drugs would target cancer cells, which are dividing exponentially. Other cells–for exam-

After a round of chemo, the patients would have dangerously low blood counts.

ple, bone marrow cells–these too would get killed. After a round of chemo, the patients would have dangerously low blood counts. They would get treatment for any infections that popped up or transfusions for anemia and be sent out again. With luck, they would replenish their bone marrow before the next round of chemotherapy. One patient I remember was Madame Simon. We called her "Madame" because she had been a French teacher in a private high school in town. She was in her late 50s. She was being treated for multiple myeloma—a blood cancer. Madame was in pain. She had cancer that had spread to her spine.

The physician with whom I was working at the time was a nice, personable young man. Madame had been his French teacher in high school. He would go out of his way to spend time with her. He would chat about school and try to make sure she was as comfortable as possible. She spent a month in the Cancer Center. Nothing was helping. We kept her on pain meds. She drifted into a comalike state and died. My colleague took it hard. He was young enough and new enough to doctoring that he had not yet built up strategies for emotional distancing.

Most patients in the Cancer Unit died–despite the beautifully appointed rooms.

I remember that during these months of taking care of really sick people, it was helpful for me to go home in the evenings and spend time with my family. I was bolstered by the Sturm und Drang of a teenage daughter's life and by taking care of a four-year-old daughter as well.

genetics and cancer
Cancer is still the "great equalizer" among diseases.

In the 1980s, I was working in a genetics lab. We were studying genes as best we could. We firmly understood the Central Dogma of Genetics: the DNA helix encodes proteins—via the intermediary of mRNA. The proteins are what drive all the cellular processes upon which bacteria and yeast and plants and mammals depend.

We knew there were 46 chromosomes in a human cell. We knew the genes were strung along the chromosomes. We were trying to figure out which gene went where in the scheme of chromosomes. "How do I map a given gene to its proper address on the 23 pairs of human chromosomes?"

We did not know what caused cancer cells to grow out of the bounds of normal cellular controls, and why they grew exponentially when normal cells divide at a dignified pace. We did not know what caused cancer, whether it was a genetic mutation or a viral infection.

That was then ... this is now. There has been a sea change in the field of genetics since those days. A major change was the firm understanding that cancer arises from genetic mutation, and that there are key genes that control the pace at which normal cells divide. These genes can undergo damage, such that they lose their normal function.

If that happens, the cell cycle and cell division are no longer restrained. A cell that has undergone this mutation will grow and divide aggressively. The mutated cell gives rise to a clone, which leads to thousands or millions of descendant cells, each with the same mutation.

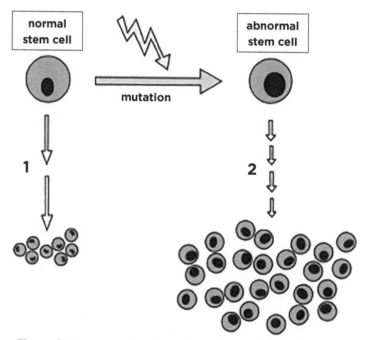

Figure 6. Bone marrow stem cells and the origin of a cancer

1. Normal cell cycling, yielding a finite number of mature cells. These are functional neutrophils, part of the immune system.

2. Mutational event causes overly-rapid cell cycling, yielding innumerable, large, immature cells. These are cancer cells (multiple myeloma in above example).

Genetics took on the heady responsibility of explaining how cancers arise. The pace of new information has been startling. Scientists now know of hundreds of genes involved in the cell cycle that give rise to cancer when mutated. We also understand how to study an individual cancer, identify which gene or genes have been tweaked, and perhaps design a targeted viral vector to attack the cancer cells.

This may go down in history as the Age of Genetics given how much we have learned in just the space of my lifetime. Cancer is still the "great equalizer" among diseases. Cancer can strike anyone, of any socioeconomic class. In fact, if you live long enough, it is almost certain you will develop a cancer. It is the price you pay for sixty or eighty years of somatic cells replicating. At some point, an error occurs in the replication process and voilà, you develop cancer.

This thought does not seem to comfort my patients when I share it. One elderly lady was 92 and had just been diagnosed with kidney cancer. She was under treatment and doing okay. When I told her cancer was the price humans pay for living into their nineties, she was not comforted.

Local Color
not every day involved sickness
One of the highlights of the year is the Blueberry Festival.

Once a year, Dry Lick holds the county fair. In the heat of a July afternoon, a parade of John Deere tractors winds through the streets. The green-and-yellow tractors cost a fortune and are the pride and joy of those who own them. Then the town fire truck and the volunteer firemen come down the street. The town's two police cars and three policemen follow behind. Finally, there is the crowning of the high school girl who has won the title of *Miss Blueberry* for the year. After the parade concludes, a street party starts, complete with a raucous band and dancing in the street.

There is, of course, the carnival that has come to town, complete with carousel and roller coaster for the small children. There are even carnies who flirt madly with the girls in town. A festive time is had by all.

The next day at the clinic, I treat the injured. A lady has pulled out her back after dancing so much at the festival. The town sheriff, who was the recipient of a bean bag toss while balanced precariously on a bucket, lost his balance and lands in a bucket of water underneath. He is diagnosed with a bruise to his tailbone that heals up in no time.

Local Color

Drama of another sort happens at the psych ward on Halloween.

The psych ward is part of the hospital down the street. They have an adolescent unit. One 16-year-old boy is acting out in the ward. He is getting belligerent and oppositional. Usually, they call the sturdy male nurses to settle down such a situation. The overhead PA system announces: "Assistance required in Psych East."

This incident takes place on Halloween Day. The nurse who answers the page for help is a hefty man who stands over six feet tall. He looks remarkably like Lieutenant Warf from

Star Trek-Enterprise. He is wearing a mask with the deeply-ridged forehead creases of Warf, along with the Star Trek uniform. He is an impressive figure. He, of course, is dressed up for the staff Halloween party that afternoon.

The young patient gets tackled by the Warf look-alike. The young man is in no condition to differentiate between a pretend and a real Warf. The patient is already in the hospital for psychiatric problems.

"Holy shit! Where did Warf come from?" the patient asks.

The patient is amazed at the hospital's ability to get Warf to come in and personally handle his takedown. He is given a tranquilizer and things improve from there.

CHAPTER EIGHT

everyday courage

The other thing I saw in practice:
how resilient people are, and how they deal with serious illness
with grace and strength. This is what I call "everyday courage."

The following two stories exemplify a trait that I call everyday courage.. The first is about Huntington's disease and the pain of watching one's spouse fall victim to its vicious effects. The second is about a gentle man's heroic battle with cancer.

huntington's chorea and the vengeful husband

Ellie Deer is a 43-year-old woman who is bright and attractive. When I first meet her, she is working as a nurse. She and her husband are raising a daughter, who is about twelve when this chapter of their lives is getting underway.

Ellie tells me she is afraid her husband is showing signs of Huntington's disease. She had known his mother, who had died of Huntington's some years before. Now she is watching her husband develop the same telltale movements she had seen in her mother-in-law, specifically, uncontrolled spasms of his arms. This is terribly upsetting to her. She has scheduled him to see a specialist, to learn what could be done to control the disease's progression, and to see what medicines might help.

I see Ellie for regular visits in the clinic. Some months later, she tells me his movements are getting worse and that the medicine isn't helping. Her husband is also becoming emotionally volatile. She is trying to be caring and supportive.

The next time I see her, she tells me his behavior is becoming more erratic—and even dangerous. He has started threatening her with ongoing outbursts of anger and physical abuse. She is becoming afraid for herself and their daughter.

Things take a turn for the worse. On the next visit, she tells me he threatened her life, and she is leaving him. She seeks a divorce and gets one, moving her daughter to a new house.

Ellie eventually gets her life back together.

But that is not the end of the saga. Dry Lick is still a small town, and a divorce does not take the husband out of their lives. The judge in divorce court has given the husband custody of the daughter on the weekends. The husband's behavior now is becoming ever more paranoid and erratic.

I draft a letter to the judge, explaining that the now ex-husband has Huntington's disease. I explain that he is entering the later phase of the disease, with manifestations of paranoia and violent behavior. I contend that he should not have custody of the child. I also add that he should never have had custody of the child in the first place.

Ellie eventually gets her life back together. The mother and daughter repair their relationship. The mother reclaims her life. The father's Huntington's worsens and eventually he leaves town to live with relatives in Ohio.

discussion of huntington's disease

Huntington's disease has been a known diagnosis since 1840. It often runs in families. A parent seems normal until age 40 or so and then starts developing abnormal movements—uncontrolled twitching of the arms and legs. These movements are called "chorea." Huntington's chorea is the other name for this syndrome. These abnormal movements are a sign that the part of the brain responsible for controlling movement is being affected.

After another year or so, cognitive changes develop. Huntington's patients develop problems with impulse control, abstract thinking, and memory. Eventually, over the space of a decade or so, dementia develops.

Aggressive behavior and compulsive behavior develop in a fair number of affected individuals. The Huntington's patient in the above story is typical for someone with the disease; onset in their 40s, heralded by abnormal body movements, and then progressing into antisocial behavior.

The disease is caused by a gene mutation. It is autosomal dominant, which means that it is passed on from parent to child. The parent can be either a mother or father. The gene mutation is not uncommon in the British Isles. It was carried over the Atlantic with early settlers and shows up with some frequency in the Scotch-Irish population who settled in Appalachia in the 1700s.

The patient did not have a biological child with her husband. They had adopted their daughter. This was a good thing. Any biological child of her husband would have a 50% risk of developing the disease. This is a frightening burden for anyone to carry.

There is now a DNA test to identify those who have inherited the gene. Many at-risk people who have watched a parent get sick with HD refuse to get the DNA test themselves. They feel it is better NOT to know whether they are doomed to the same fate as their parent.

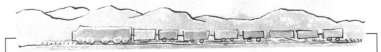

two things this patient taught me:

1. *Judges are not familiar with medical conditions like Huntington's disease. The judge should have believed her when she said her husband was becoming paranoid and violent.*

2. *Admiration for the enormous mental strength and determination of my patient. Ellie managed to leave a dangerous situation and to make a new life for herself and her daughter. She taught me how strong people can be. That they can come through horrific experiences and still find the strength to go on.*

the steady postman

Mike Callahan is a 75-year-old retired post office worker. I have known him for nine years. His medical issues were the usual for the first two years I knew him. He had bypass surgery for heart blockages at age 65, but otherwise he was doing fine.

Seven years ago, however, his health took a turn for the worse. He presented to the emergency room, complaining, "I am short of breath." A chest X-ray revealed a mass on the left side of his chest. This turned out to be multiple myeloma, a type of cancer.

Chemotherapy is the next step. The treatment is intense. The cancer responds to the chemo and goes into remission. Then the side effects of chemo appear: he develops pain in his legs due to nerve damage and requires strong pain medicine. He starts medicines for anxiety and depression.

I call this the "everyday courage."

At the time of this clinic visit, he complains, "I have been sick to my stomach for the last five days." He feels light-headed, and he is eating little. The cancer clinic refuses to give him chemo that day because he is so weak and nauseated. He appears pale and frail. His gait is unsteady. He needs intravenous fluids for dehydration and medicines for nausea.

I think of him as a brave man. He deals stoically with the chemo —and then with the side effects of chemo. He survives seven years with a serious illness. Multiple myeloma is a harsh diagnosis.

I watch as he loses weight and as he deals with leg pain. But he is always upbeat in the clinic and sanguine about what hand he has been dealt. I see this repeatedly with different patients. I call this the "everyday courage."

He dies shortly after this clinic visit.

what this case taught me:

"Everyday courage." People are marvelously adaptable. They deal with whatever life hands them. They have no choice. They make hard decisions. They face death with some modicum of calmness. The pain of their illness probably makes the descent into death less scary. Perhaps it is a welcome alternative to continued suffering; I do not know.

Still, I saw people gracefully accommodating to whatever changes they must make. I watched them adjusting to new situations and making life changes. Not quickly, not without tears, but over time.

CHAPTER NINE

handsome men and the plasticity of gender

*In popular culture, the beautiful man is invariably
the star of the movie, whether it be a romance or an adventure.*

This chapter contains some comments on male beauty and the expectations that travel with it. Then further comments on gender plasticity: how the body template starts off as androgynous and is tweaked into the male direction only if testosterone is present. Then a discussion of transgender patients and the challenges they present.

the beautiful man
What life events had brought him to a psych hospital?

Eric Condor is being admitted to the psych ward at the VA because he is acting out and suicidal. I am a medical student doing a rotation through the VA inpatient psych ward. There was a sorting ritual for who got the most fun rotation. And I literally drew the short end of the stick, landing the least desirable rotation.

My mission as a med student is to perform the initial intake exam. I observe a young man in exam room one, ready for his physical exam. I notice, due to my excellent observational skills, that he is buck naked.

I note that his gluteus maximus muscles are well delineated, as are his latissimus dorsi. This is my first patient exam in the psych unit and apparently buck naked is the standard.

After my initial shock wears off, I try to regain the full measure of seriousness at my disposal. I proceed to perform a professional-level intake exam to the best of my newly-minted abilities. The patient is a 27-year-old white male in excellent physical condition. He is also remarkably handsome. That is about the sum total of my exam.

He is then allowed to get dressed. We proceed to stage two of the intake exam. Why was he here? What life events had brought him to a psych hospital?

His story is riveting. He worked on a naval carrier. He describes in great detail how his job was to signal the planes as they came in for a landing on the deck of the carrier. One day, a plane crashes as it lands. The plane veers off course and strikes another sailor on the deck. And this sailor is decapitated. The patient relates this story with fresh horror, even though it had happened a year before.

He finished his tour of duty and returned to civilian life, working in construction. He then acquired a girlfriend, who was the daughter of a wealthy lawyer. She broke up with him after two months. The breakup triggered the deep depression that currently has him in its grip.

If life were a Hollywood movie, someone this attractive would play the hero who saves the planet from invading aliens.

I can easily imagine this young woman finding him a likely mate. He is way off the scale of male good looks. If life were a Hollywood movie, someone this attractive would play the hero who saves the planet from invading aliens.

The next test involves intellectual and mental health questions. There is a series of questions regarding common sayings and aphorisms. The patient is asked to explain what the following phrases mean:

The early bird catches the worm.
Make hay while the sun shines.

His answers are unexpected. In each case, he interprets the phrase literally. He explains that worms are most active in the morning and that's why the early bird catches the worm. He informs me that hay must be harvested and baled in dry, sunny weather or else it molds.

My patient, as it turns out, worked on a farm throughout his growing-up years. He is also the most concrete thinker I have ever met. He is unable to see a metaphor when it hits him in the face.

Answers to other questions I ask him are also revealing. The patient left high school early after doing poorly in school. This beautiful young man is not particularly bright.

I can understand why his girlfriend had left him. Her handsome young man is not intellectually stimulating and a bit on the dull side. He is, no doubt, not up to the standards of her social set.

My heart goes out to him because he has no way of understanding any of this.

In the next few weeks, for the time he was an inpatient, he continues to relive the trauma of the carrier crash. The formal diagnosis is post-traumatic stress disorder, which is a common finding among vets in the psych unit. I continue to be supportive when I see him.

He stabilizes on meds and is discharged from the hospital. He is planning to leave the big city and go back to the small town where he grew up on the farm. I am guessing he found a better fit in his farming community than in the big city.

what I learned:

In popular culture, the beautiful man is invariably the star of the movie, whether it be a romance or an adventure. He is always intelligent, daring, and decisive. This patient, however, had none of these attributes, but he was beautiful.

The young woman in his life took him on as a boyfriend, no doubt, because he looked the part of the perfect boyfriend. She probably learned his limitations over time. Without the burden of beauty, maybe he would have found a less-stellar girlfriend and been happier. The girlfriend from a wealthy family broke up with him, which contributed to his breakdown and stay in the psychiatric unit. He needed to find someone was more a match to his simplicity.

another handsome man
I am well aware of the plasticity of gender.

Jamie Stewart is another handsome young man. He sports a full beard, as well as lots of fur on his chest and legs, and speaks in a deep voice. He complains of a bladder infection.

Now, young men rarely get bladder infections. Men's plumbing is protective by design. The male urinary tract is elongated, and bacteria have a difficult time climbing in from the outside to the inside. The urethra is a good ten inches long, for heaven's sake. The comparable distance for a woman's anatomy is only an inch or two. That means very little effort at all for bacteria on the outside to travel an inch or two to the inside of a woman and and set up shop as a bladder infection.

When this young man presents to the clinic claiming another bladder infection, I cannot help my skepticism. Much to my surprise, the test of his urine does show an infection. His symptoms and his gender do not add up to the number of infections he's encountering.

I sweep into the exam room with my medical scribe in tow. The scribe is a young woman who is new to the medical field but learning fast. Her mission is to

My young scribe fails to keep a blank face.

keep a blank face and show no reaction whatsoever to whatever transpires in the clinic room. She is just supposed to record for the electronic medical record.

As I return to the exam room after the urine test, aware that something was not as it seemed, this young man explains. "You are probably wondering how I could get a bladder infection," he says. "I've gotten them before, not infrequently. You see, while I look like a man, my genitals are those of a female. I am on testosterone, which explains why I look like a man. My male partner and I have had to deal with these bladder infections several times in the past year."

My young scribe fails to keep a blank face. Her eyes get noticeably big and round, and she looks like she is going to ask him if he's really a woman.

She manages not to say anything out loud. I tell the patient his response to testosterone is quite impressive. I never would have guessed he is transgender. I write a prescription for an antibiotic. He thanks me and leaves.

At that point, once the patient leaves the clinic, my scribe is incredulous. "He looks like a man," she says. "I never would have guessed he was a woman!" She continues with other exclamations along the same vein.

This is fun for me to watch. As a doctor, I have met other transgender people. I am already well aware of the plasticity of gender.

Embryonic plasticity. We all start life as an embryo, neither male nor female. We have primitive parts. If a primitive gonad gets the message (the presence of the Y chromosome) that it belongs to a would-be male and starts going in the direction of a testicle, then testosterone is produced and sweeps the fetal body.

Under its influence, the primordial male tubules develop into the internal genitalia of the male, with the gonads migrating through the lower body and settling into the formative scrotum. Under the influence of testosterone, external genitalia develop as well. The baby develops a penis, with the scrotal sacs housing the testicles.

If that pulse of testosterone is absent, if the baby is a would-be girl or if the signals that allow testosterone to be detected are absent, then the primordial plumbing goes in the female direction. The baby develops female pattern anatomy. The little gonads stay put inside the abdomen and turn into ovaries. The female tubules shown below turn into Fallopian tubes and a uterus. The external genitalia turn into a clitoris and vagina.

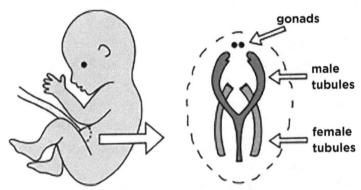

Figure 7. 8-week human fetus:
With both male and female parts

I take this sequence of events personally. The primordial template is female. I find this intriguing. The female template is the default position. In the absence of the testosterone, all fetuses go in the female pattern. I first studied embryology in college. It was during a time in this country when we were discussing sexism and feminism and the differences between men and women. It was 1973—quite a tumultuous time. I found it informative that the differences between the sexes were not that dramatic. The embryo starts off with the default position of "female" and only leaves that position if something happens, e.g., a testosterone pulse. It means the two sexes are not that different after all. And that females rule.

In the transgender individual, let us say that this individual is a biologic female (e.g., this patient), and she decides that her true destiny is to transition to a male. It's not that hard ... just take lots of testosterone. The skin cells and hair follicles are sensitive to hormones. If testosterone is present, body hair develops in a male pattern. The muscles are sensitive to hormones. If testosterone is present, muscle mass increases. The voice box changes. The voice gets deeper. Voilà! Your appearance is that of a normal male person except for the genitalia. They remain female.

It is not magic. It is just hormones.

the other transition:
from male to female

Stephanie Watkins arrives at the clinic. The nurse's note states that the patient is a 29-year-old female here for an annual exam. When I enter the exam room, I see a very tall young woman. She has a thick head of curly hair and wearing lots of makeup and a stylist dress. She is easily is six feet tall. Her voice is a bit low, a bit husky. She confirms that she is here for her an annual exam.

Just for the record, the height of the patient and the exuberance of the hairstyle did make me wonder if she was a male wearing a wig and a dress. But I was not going to say as much.

For female patients, "annual exam" usually means a "pelvic exam." Young women come in every couple of years for a refill on birth control pills, or for an STD check. They get a vaginal exam with a speculum to make sure they don't have any STDs. I ask this young person if she is needing a vaginal exam.

She looks horrified.

Stephanie appears very confused. I must show her what a speculum looks like and explain what happens during a pelvic exam.

She looks horrified and then tells me, "I have male parts down below!" This certainly explains why she is so very tall.

I feel just a bit foolish for not having asked her if she was a man. Either way, it would have been a difficult conversation. People who are transgender get offended if you guess the gender they are trying to leave behind. In my experience, it is a no-win conversation.

It turns out, Stephanie was previously known as Stephen and is in transition from male to female. She has started taking estrogen pills and wants further guidance on what other meds she should take. I refer her to a clinic that specializes in hormonal treatments for those who are transitioning.

Hormones for the transition from male to female mostly involves estrogen. Again, secondary sex characteristics are controlled by the hormonal environment. If one decreases levels of testosterone, then the balance goes toward the female appearance. And certainly, if you throw in a sufficient amount of estrogen, the process speeds along.

There are three ways to decrease testosterone levels:

1. surgical castration—removal of the testicles
2. medicines that block the production of testosterone; and
3. estrogen, the female hormone.

Estrogen has an anti-testosterone effect and promotes a more feminine appearance.

In the absence of testosterone, and certainly in the presence of estrogen, the breasts develop; the skin becomes softer; muscle mass decreases; and body hair decreases.

Contrary to what many believe, most men in transition do not opt for castration. Hormonal treatments are straightforward and reliable.

CHAPTER TEN

doctor speak

*I had visions of Satan and demons
and who knew what else.*

The following is an introduction to "doctor speak": terms that doctors routinely use or misuse. Often, doctor language is obscure. Sometimes the obscurity is intentional. See the expression "surgical misadventure" below. Sometimes the obscurity is hard-baked into medicine, as the profession continues to use Greek and Latin names for body parts and for diseases. Finally, doctor terms show the wry sense of humor that doctors and nurses cultivate to survive. See the expression "celestial discharge."

I hope you enjoy your tour of doctor speak. It may help you translate what it is your doctor or provider is trying to say.

satanic value

My son was born. He was orange in color, but otherwise healthy. He had a routine newborn lab test, checking for levels of bilirubin. The baby's liver kicks into action at two to three days of age and starts processing bilirubin (a normal breakdown product of red blood cells). Sometimes the liver fails to activate, and the baby builds up an excess of bilirubin and keeps an orange-yellow color in his skin. That's what my little baby was doing: staying orange.

The lab called me with the result. The young voice on the other end of the phone line said, "The baby's bilirubin came back. It is high. It is a satanic value!" I had visions of Satan and demons and who knew what else. It took me a few seconds to translate what she meant to say. The correct term is "panic value." Yes, his bili levels were high. It took another two months for them to normalize. But he was not possessed by a devil. How comforting.

how to speak like a doctor

You do not know what your doctor is talking about,
which is handy for your doctor.

- Your illness is *idiopathic*. This means doctors have no idea what triggered your illness. We do not know the cause. It is just one of those things that pops up for no reason known to doctors.

- This is in contradistinction to *iatrogenic*. The statement "your illness is iatrogenic" carries a vastly different meaning.

  It means it was triggered by something your doctor did. Perhaps it was a medicine prescribed that caused an adverse reaction or a surgery gone awry. Or maybe the surgeon accidently clipped the nerves

  It means he has gone to heaven.

  to your bladder, which is why you can no longer control your bladder.

- By the way, the word for surgery gone awry is *surgical misadventure*.

- *Psychosomatic* means your doctor thinks you are making it up. This is almost invariably applied to a female patient. You are told, "You have a headache (or stomach pain) because you are stressed." Rather than the doctor taking your complaint seriously, he or she goes to a default position and assumes you are over-reacting to everyday stress. It takes longer for a female to be diagnosed with serious causes for a headache or for stomach pain because of the longstanding tradition of discounting women's complaints.

• Medicine is chockful of Greek and Latin words. *Hyperthyroidism* means your thyroid is pumping out too much hormone. *Hypo* means too little. The heart is called *cardio*. The lungs are called *pulmonary*. A kidney stone is a *nephrolithiasis*. It means kidney stone inflammation. A kidney infection is *pyelonephritis*.

What is the goal of everything being in Greek or Latin? When medicine was codified, it was based on Greek or Latin medical books from 2,000 years ago. The upshot right now is that you do not know what your doctor is talking about, which is handy for your doctor because he or she can use these words and keep you mystified.

• "Celestial discharge." You ask the nurse, "Where is Mr. Smith in bed three?" She tells you he has either been discharged home or transferred to the Intensive Care Unit. A third response could be that he has had a "celestial discharge."

The latter is not good. It means he has died and gone to heaven.

CHAPTER ELEVEN

September 11, 2001, and its aftermath

A doctor from India had been forced off a public bus in eastern Kentucky because he looked like he was Muslim.

The falling of the Twin Towers affected our small town; its ripples in eastern Kentucky, and its long-term health effects on first responders.

September 11, 2001

I am in a meeting at 9:15 a.m. at the hospital. The head of the hospital is leading the meeting. His phone rings. He picks it up and says, "What? A plane flew into the World Trade Center? That makes no sense!"

A few minutes later, his informant calls again. This time, he shares the news of a second plane flying into the other tower. The meeting comes to a close. We part ways, deeply confused, and concerned as to what is happening.

I am en route to the clinic. I pass a TV. It is showing clips of planes flying into the Twin Towers. Ultimately, it is showing the collapse of one tower. A few minutes later, it shows the collapse of the second tower. I am aghast. I understand there are 50,000 people in the towers.

I am still in shock when I arrive at the clinic. I have a patient in the exam room waiting to see me. I take a few minutes to gather my thoughts. When I finally see my patient, I am still unable to keep my anxiety at bay. I blurt out the news to the patient.

"The Twin Towers in New York are falling!" I exclaim. "There are thousands of people in there!"

My patient is a woman in her 50s. She is due for a refill on anxiety meds. Thank goodness she was still medicated while I shared my disturbing message. Her morning dose of Xanax kept her from responding adversely to my blast of anxiety.

"Oh, I hope they are okay," the patient responds. "What I am here for is my refill."

We went on from there.

I learn within another few minutes that there is *not* a full complement of people in the Towers. There were only around 3,000 people who had come to work early before the usual 9 a.m. start time. The tragedy is still enormous.

No one wants to look like or sound like a Middle Easterner.

The patient leaves. The staff gathers in the front office. We listen to the radio, which was telling us about the attack on New York. It said other towers across the country were being evacuated in case this was part of a larger attack.

I thought of my sister in Cleveland. Her office was near the Terminal Tower, the tallest building in the city. Other clinic staff were worried about the Sears Tower in Chicago, where they also had family. All planes in the country were grounded. No flights were allowed for the next two days or so.

The next day was a Wednesday. Eastern Kentucky is my destination to cover a shift in a clinic that is deep in the mountains. No one wants to look like or sound like they a Middle Easterner. We all understood that Islamic militants had orchestrated this attack. In my drive to the clinic, I believe I wore a Jewish star during that drive through the mountains just in case I was pulled over by overzealous police.

My fears of being mistaken for an Islamic militant were not completely unfounded. In the newspaper the next week, they reported that a doctor from India had been forced off a public bus in eastern Kentucky because he looked like he was Muslim. He had brown skin, but he was, in fact, Hindu. India had fought a big civil war to make sure the Hindus stayed in India and the Muslims moved to soon-to-be Pakistan.

Why did so many Indian and Pakistani doctors come to practice in our communities of Appalachia?

A large percentage of the physician force in the small towns of Appalachia were doctors who were born in India or Pakistan. A fair number were from Indonesia as well. Why did so many Indian and Pakistani doctors come to practice in our communities of Appalachia? The answer was quite simple: these doctors came to these small towns because they needed green cards and permission to stay in this country.

We had a coterie of five Pakistani doctors working with us in Dry Lick. They were all called Mohammed. You had to call them by their last names because the first name did not help in the least. They prayed as a group every Friday. They were all family men with wives and children.

The wives were all well-educated, with advanced degrees. Apparently, high-class families in Pakistan arrange marriages for their sons with women who are also accomplished.

However, one doctor was not from such an elevated stratum of society. He was darker in skin tone and shorter than the others. He said it was harder for him to get a wife, but he finally succeeded.

The most handsome doctor from Pakistan was a surgeon. He was from a high social class back in Pakistan. Others were internists. The surgeon had married his first cousin. This was a preferred marriage for his social class. They all had lovely children. They were all good doctors. We were fortunate to have them in town. They all finished their obligatory tenure in an underserved area. Those who could, moved to practice in Florida. This apparently is the equivalent of Mecca if you are an internist.

I hope, after the mayhem of the Towers falling in New York and the beginning of our national campaign against Muslims, that our five doctors did well in their careers. And I hope they got to take care of rich retirees in Florida.

the blue man

I meet Mr. McCarthy some years after the Towers fall. He is a 45-year-old stocky guy. He is pleasant in demeanor and talkative. He has blue eyes and red hair.

He is also blue. His lips are blue in color, his hands and feet are blue. He is not related to the blue family with the double recessive gene mention in an earlier chapter.

He reports that he has lung disease and has had trouble breathing for some years now. Originally, he was a coal miner in Tennessee and later became a firefighter at some point. He was one of the first responders when the Twin Towers fell in New York on 9/11.

It is not my imagination that this patient is blue.

Mr. McCarthy has now developed a complex lung disease, some combination of coal miner's lungs and damage from the detritus at the Twin Towers site. His blue color is from lack of oxygen. His lungs are not providing enough oxygen to his bloodstream.

He says he needs admission to the hospital for diuretics, to take off the extra fluid and needs oxygen. He reveals that when he gets blue like this, his legs swell up.

The reason his legs swell up is because he has heart damage in addition to lung damage and fibrosis. This is secondary to the scarring and increased pressure in the lungs. The heart damage makes the heart pump extra hard to get deoxygenated blood into the pulmonary arteries. It is working so hard, it gets overwhelmed and loses its ability to pump at full capacity. Mr. McCarthy has congestive heart failure.

So, it is not my imagination that this patient is blue. His oxygen levels are in the low 80s. A normal oxygen level is 96%. His blood is lacking the oxygen bump it was supposed to pick up on its transit through the lungs. Without the oxygen bolus, his blood is bluer than it should be.

His cardiologist is fully prepared to bring him in again and he is hospitalized. He is given a cocktail of diuretics to help pull off the excess fluid on board along with supplementary oxygen. This is repeated every few weeks when his daily regimen of meds needs to be tweaked.

He dies at 47 leaving behind a wife and two daughters.

MEDICAL BACKGROUND: Lung disease and heart failure.
He had lung damage due to toxic exposures: coal dust, and the debris and dust from the fall of the Twin Towers. He had swollen legs from secondary damage to his heart.

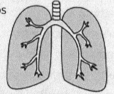

The heart is a double pump. One side pumps deoxygenated blood to the lungs, to pick up fresh oxygen. If the heart must pump against high pressure—for example, fibrosis in the lungs—then it has to work a lot harder than usual. At some point, it can no longer keep up with its workload. That is called right heart failure. Because of pump failure, blood and fluids pool in the legs.

It is basically a plumbing problem. For example, homeowners have a sump pump in the basement. The sump pump fails, and three feet of water collect in the basement. That is why the patient's legs would swell up at times. Pulling off some of the excess fluid with diuretics helps because it decreases the workload of a heart that is working past its capacity to recover some of its function.

what this teaches me:

Lung damage in coal miners is a known entity.
The exposures of the first responders at the Twin Towers
site has also caused a plague of lung disease and
the deaths of thousands of young men and women.

a personal note

The towers fell on September 11, 2001. I had just been in New York City no more than four weeks before on a family vacation. We stayed on the Upper West Side in a nice hotel overlooking the Museum of Natural History. We had our two kids with us, ages 9 and 13. Their interest in the museum was lukewarm. We spent time taking cabs and tours to sites in the heart of Manhattan. One day, we took the ferry to the Statue of Liberty. The next day, we went to the top of the Empire State Building. I had gone there as a child and remembered being thrilled by the view. This was the third time I had been back to the viewing deck on the 72nd floor. I was not quite as thrilled as I had been decades before.

We took a double decker bus tour around the harbor area and through the streets of Chinatown. I remember it was hot and noisy and the traffic was terrible. We were supposed to go to the top of the Twin Towers. I was tired and cranky and said we can put it off until the next day. I

Who knew it would become a symbol of the Time Before.

wanted to get back to the peace and quiet of the hotel. The kids put up no resistance whatsoever.

It turns out our trip was cut short. I had to get back earlier than anticipated, back to work in Kentucky. We never made it to the top of the World Trade Center. I thought we could see it another time, the next time we visited New York.

That obviously did not happen. I still have the snow globe we bought on that trip, with the skyline of New York showing the Empire State Building and the Twin Towers. Who knew it would become a symbol of the Time Before.

CHAPTER TWELVE

lessons from the ER

Do not, as a physician, believe an unlikely story.

My patients have taught me many things.

✓ They have taught me how to deal with a poor hand when it comes to absent thumbs or damaged balance and cerebellar damage.

✓ They have taught me how a young girl develops into a mother.

✓ They have taught me how a middle-aged man deals with heart failure after working at the Twin Towers site.

Besides seeing patients in the clinic, I also covered the Emergency Room in the local little hospital up the road. I saw interesting and sometimes amusing patients there. Three amusing patients are described below. They come in two flavors: drunk stupid or plain stupid.

There are ER stories that follow, more serious than the first three: the patient who was seriously ill and had no health insurance, and the young man under police escort.

threesome from the ER

Drunk stupid #1. The first patient is a 40-year-old fellow who is mildly intoxicated. He is brought to the ER by a woman friend. He lifts his leg up on the exam table.

"I shot myself in the leg," he says. "I was cleaning out my pellet gun. It accidentally went off and got me in the thigh."

There are many puncture wounds in the quadriceps muscle, along the front of his right thigh. The X-ray shows around 100 pellets, all embedded fairly deep into the muscle. I counted them. The woman friend keeping him company in the ER does not say a word.

Never underestimate the stupidity of the situation.

It turns out he had been more than a little drunk earlier that evening. He had been, in his inebriated state, fooling around with someone else's girlfriend. The someone else had shot him; now the patient is trying to cover up for the someone else. The police get involved.

what I learned:

It is inadvisable to get drunk and flirt with someone else's girlfriend, especially if there is a pellet rifle involved. Even though my patient sobered up remarkably in the ER and maintained his story, do not, as a physician, believe an unlikely story.

Drunk stupid #2. The second patient is a 20-year-old male who comes to the ER with his drinking buddies after a Saturday night spent drinking beer at a lake.

"I decided to jump from the cliff into the water. Water was shallow, who knew?" he says.

The patient broke both his feet, according to X-rays. He has fractures of both calcaneus bones, i.e., the heel bones. It is extremely difficult to fracture this bone.

what this patient taught me:

Twenty-year-old males do a lot of silly things when they are drunk. And they often get drunk. If they can make it to age 25 without killing themselves, that is a good sign.

Plain stupid. A roly-poly fellow, somewhere in his 40s, appears in the ER in his grubby clothes from a day of wandering in the woods.

"I collect mushrooms," he says. "I thought this one might be poisonous, but I ate it anyway."

He shows me a large gray-brown mushroom, with a bite taken out of it. The mushroom is as large as a dinner plate. After his arrival in the ER, he starts vomiting. I call Poison Control. They say he just needs to throw up the offending fungus.

what this patient taught me:

Never underestimate the stupidity of the situation. The patient told me he thought the mushroom might be poisonous before he ate it. This patient also taught me that nausea with vomiting is nature's emetic, much better than what we usually give in the ER.

sick husband

*Among other things, my patients have showed me
what it is like not to have health insurance.*

I am covering the Emergency Room again and chatting with one of the nurses. She is married and has two teenagers. It is always a pleasure to catch up with her and to hear what's happening with her family.

She tells me about going to a wedding of a friend where everyone dresses in camouflage. Even the bridesmaids' dresses are made of camouflage. The dresses are accessorized with orange flip-flops. The pictures are unusual … and charming.

The family does not have health insurance.

This time, she tells me she is worried about her husband. He is a generally healthy construction worker in his mid-40s. He has gotten sick in the last six months. She shares that he complains of constant stomach pains, throws up a lot, and he has lost fifty pounds.

When I asked what they had done, she surprised me with the response. "We are saving up money to see a stomach specialist. The doctor at our small rural ER saw him a month ago and recommended a stomach specialist."

The family does not have health insurance. This is in the days before Obamacare. Many families in town try to play the odds and get by without having to spend $500 or $1,000 per month for health insurance. This family, though, apparently lost the lottery. When the husband got sick, they have no affordable access to health care, other than the Emergency Room.

His pain is unbearable, and I do what I can to mediate it.

Our little rural hospital had a grant such that we could see patients in the ER and not have to charge them for the visit. The federal government picked up the cost. When her husband came to the ER one month before, the ER doctor sent him for a CT scan just down the hall from the ER, so he wouldn't incur the cost.

The CT scan had been read as normal. It did not show any evidence of cancer or of infection. The ER doctor at that visit told the family that the husband needs to see a stomach specialist.

So, now I have the back story on the husband's health troubles. The next shift I cover, he comes into the ER. He is throwing up nonstop now and has lost even more weight. His pain is unbearable, and I do what I can to mediate it. A call is placed to the ER at the Big City Hospital and an ambulance is called to transport him. The pain he is experiencing is a dire sign.

He sees the stomach specialist and gets an endoscopy that day. As I expected, they find a large stomach cancer. The original CT scan missed it because the density of normal and abnormal tissue looked the same on the scanner. He is hospitalized for several days and started on chemotherapy and seems to be doing better. Weight is even gained.

Then four months later, he complains of severe low back pain. It turns out the cancer has spread to his spine. He dies within three days.

what this case taught me:

How unfair our medical system is for many people.
This is a working man. He always worked to support his
family. Like many families in town, he could not afford health
insurance. He got what medical care he could from the ER.
But the care is haphazard. He could not afford the definitive
testing and specialist referrals. Then he died.

Maybe, if it had been diagnosed early, he could have survived. I do not know. What I do know is that he needed better care.

taser time

Being a doctor in a small town, I, of course, got to know the patients well. I also got to know the police in town, especially with covering the Emergency Room. The police would often be the ones bringing in a patient or someone they arrested for treatment.

There is a young man in bed #1 in the ER. He is drunk as a skunk, as they say. He is also in police custody, with handcuffs on during the exam. The police are bringing him into the ER and not treating him all that kindly. He is combative and keeps trying to get away. He is too drunk to realize that an escape was not going to happen, what with two policemen standing nearby. One of them holds a Taser.

"Go on, keep giving us trouble. I would be delighted to tase you, buddy!" the police officer barks.

Now that seemed harsh on the face of it. But I am in total agreement with the police officer on this one.

The back story: In bed #3, on the other side of the ER, is his girlfriend. She is seven months pregnant. The young man had apparently kept her locked up in his house for the preceding three days. Somehow, she had gotten away and called the police. The police had brought the two of them into the ER. She needed attention for the bruises on her face. He needed a decision on how drunk he was and whether he should be kept overnight in the hospital for detox. I had examined the girlfriend first. She was pretty shaken. She was young, no more than 23 years old.

When I see the police officer taunting the young abusive man, I was hoping he would start acting up and they would tase him. I believed everyone in the ER was angry with this ne'er-do-well. We all would have applauded.

The young man went to jail for domestic abuse. The young woman went to her mother's house.

CHAPTER THIRTEEN

deep in the mountains

Every family in this eastern Kentucky town
had lost at least one family member.

I would sometimes work in another town, helping to cover a clinic deep in the mountains of eastern Kentucky. It was a rougher community than the town where I usually worked. During my time there, I saw the devastating toll that opioid addiction takes on a community.

The opioid epidemic was just taking hold in eastern Kentucky. There was no work for young people in town. The coal mines were closing, there was no manufacturing nearby, and there were no factory jobs. Either you worked for the city as a teacher, or you worked at the hospital. The young people who stayed in town were often making a living off the drug trade.

Drug dealers would drive down I-65 to the drug clinics that were proliferating all over Florida. They could get prescriptions for hundreds of Lortabs or Percocets or Oxycodones or Xanax. They would purchase the drugs, then drive back to Kentucky along I-65.

Sometimes the drug dealers partook of their own supply and overdosed alongside the highway. They didn't always make it back safely to town. If they did return, they could sell their stash for a hefty profit—while keeping some, of course, for their own use.

Every family in this eastern Kentucky town had lost at least one family member—whether a sibling or a cousin—to a drug overdose.

Besides two vignettes about the toll that opioid addiction has on a community, I have also included a story of a colorful patient recently released from prison. Another denizen of a rough-around-the-edges mountain community.

young woman
with a spider bite

The grandmother, as so often is the case,
ends up raising the child.

I am seeing a new patient in this clinic deep in the mountains. Melinda is a young woman in her late twenties. With dark hair and dark eyes, she is jittery and thin, too. She would have been pretty except for looking harried.

Melinda tells me she got bitten by a brown recluse spider and came to the clinic because the bite looks infected. She shows me her thigh where there is an ugly circular wound, four inches in diameter. The skin is black in color. Black is never a good color. It means necrotic skin; the skin has died.

She reveals that she got bitten a week ago. Something about seeing a spider on her bed, in between a pile of clothes, and being too stoned to worry about it at the time. She went to bed and woke up the next morning with a bite mark on her leg. She also tells me she is a drug addict.

Melinda gets back into heavy opioids.

Apparently, brown recluse spiders are not uncommon in eastern Kentucky. She had correctly identified the spider. It is a dangerous bite. The black, dead skin needs to be surgically removed. I send her to a nearby hospital for debridement and for a skin graft.

The patient returns for a follow-up visit two weeks later. The skin graft is healing, but it is taking a long time to do so. Plus, she just found out she is pregnant.

The next series of visits turn out to be a balancing act. What to do with a patient who is in pain from a partially-healed wound and is asking for pain meds versus the reality of a pregnancy that usually precludes pain meds? She ends up on anxiety meds, carefully titrated by her OB-GYN.

The baby is eventually born. Melinda gets back into heavy opioids. She overdoses and dies. The grandmother, as so often is the case, ends up raising the child.

more fall out
from the opioid epidemic
Families take care of their own in this community.

More grandparents are raising their grandchildren. The parents are either lost in the miasma of drug use, in jail, or dead. Mr. and Mrs. Watkins are examples. He is in his late 60s, a heavyset man with a voice roughened by decades of tobacco use. He works on cars a lot and keeps some degree of grease stains on his clothes.

Mrs. Watkins is a slender, hyperactive spit of a woman. She looks frazzled around the edges and looks older than 65. She works hard keeping house and taking care of the kids.

The Watkins' daughter and her husband had gotten over-involved in drugs some years before. They neglected the kids. Social Services investigated the home situation and took the kids away and put them in foster care. The grandparents asked for and received custody.

That was five years ago. The grandparents have done a good job. The girl is now ten years old, and boy is 13. They are soft-spoken and polite, well-groomed, wearing clean clothes. They are doing well in school. It is obvious they are loved and cared for.

This family stays in my thoughts because of what happens next. Mrs. Watkins gets sick with lung cancer. She wasn't a smoker, but she had lived with her husband for 45 years and been exposed to second-hand smoke. She dies.

Mr. Watkins himself is in poor health. One of their other daughters steps in and takes custody of the grandkids. Families take care of their own in this community.

In the early days of the opioid epidemic, it may well have been Appalachia that was hit the hardest. Young people were scrambling to get prescriptions for narcotics out of their primary care doctors. Grandparents stepped in and raised their grandchildren because the parents were in jail. Now it is no longer limited to Appalachia. One can find these stories anywhere across the country now. The "opioid epidemic" is nationwide and growing.

the guy with the fake eye
"What were you in jail for?" I ask conversationally.

Deep in the mountains, a rough-looking guy comes into the clinic. He is about 45 years old. He looks like a weightlifter, with a muscled torso and arms. He has tattoos all over, with nothing artistic about the ink—naked girls, weaponry, skulls. He looks scary. His right eye is fake. He tells me he lost it in a fight when he was in his twenties.

I go into my doctoring persona to avoid looking more closely at the tattoos. I ask him why he has come to the clinic He mentions needing blood pressure meds. He says he just got out of jail and needs to get refills on his meds.

For some reason, maybe from an excess of naïveté, I ask this man about his time behind bars. Most patients I have met with jail time were in for nonviolent offenses such as drug possession or DUIs.

"What were you in jail for?" I ask conversationally.

"Murder," he replies.

That pretty much puts an end to that conversational gambit. I scurry back to inquiring what refills he needs. I am eager to please him and get him quickly out the door. I am keenly aware that I did not want to get this guy angry. I write prescriptions for his blood pressure meds and virtually anything else he wants as long as it is not a controlled substance. And with a sigh of relief, I escort him to the checkout desk.

After that encounter, I never ask why patients went to jail. Not unless I have some prior knowledge of their benign nature.

CHAPTER FOURTEEN

three scourges of the south

I know, as a physician,
that there is little I can do at times.

As a transplant from the North, I am unprepared for the scourges of the South: the three diseases that run rampant in the rural south. Every day in practice, I see several patients with COPD, alcoholism, or diabetes. It seems that every family has someone affected by at least one of these diseases.

lung disease

Matt Branwell is a 47-year-old man who tells me he started smoking when he was six years old. He says he went behind the barn and rolled his own smoke. His father ran a tobacco farm. Matt helped harvest tobacco as a youngster. He has been smoking ever since that first cigarette at age six. He smokes two packs a day, and sometimes three packs a day. That is forty years of smoking!

He is thin. His color is poor. His face is crisscrossed with deep lines. He looks twenty years older than 47. He says he is getting short-winded with just walking up a small hill. His chest is thin and elongate. He has emphysema, so he stays short of breath.

Smoking cigarettes damages the elasticity of the lungs. They are unable to expand and to properly process oxygen. Matt is dealing with low oxygen routinely. It is comparable to hanging out at the base camp for an ascent of Mount Everest. Base camp is at 14,000 feet altitude.

I give him inhalers to use during the day along with oxygen to use at night. He is not supposed to use oxygen and smoke at the same time because it can cause a fire. Oxygen is flammable, after all. He will still smoke. There will be a small fire, if he is lucky; a conflagration if he is not lucky. There is no effective treatment for the level of lung disease that he has.

When he dies, at age 54, he leaves behind two grown daughters who grieve for him.

alcoholism

In his 50s, Randy Fetts is a gadabout. He contributes to the local color of the town. He hangs out with the other ne'er-do-wells on the lawn of the courthouse, where there are some nice benches, if the weather is good. Otherwise, the group of three or four hang out under the overhang that protects the front steps of an adjoining building.

Randy sports a full gray beard and long hair. He looks like an aging hippie. I see him in the clinic as a patient. He confesses he started growing the long hair and beard when he went to San Francisco for the Summer of Love in 1967. It is definitely NOT a political statement. He tells you that the look helps him get women.

He tells you he is on medicines for liver disease. He is an alcoholic and sees a liver specialist to try to control the damage done by decades of drinking.

He also gives you—unsolicited—his opinion of the local mayor and his cronies. He tells you that they are keeping a new supermarket from coming to town because it would compete with the mayor's supermarket. Randy has some strong, and probably well-informed, opinions about local politics. He grew up in this little town and has spent decades here.

Randy has quit drinking as far as I know. He is properly impressed and scared of the diagnosis of liver failure. He does well and is stable on his meds for three years. Then, after seeing him for those three years, he apparently starts drinking again. There are stories of him patronizing the liquor store at the bottom of the hill. He lives with his elderly mother, who has an old house in town at the top of the hill. He ends up in the ER and is then hospitalized.

His death is a loss for the town.

I visit him in the hospital. He is inebriated and disoriented. He goes through withdrawal. I try to modulate the intensity of withdrawal with tapering doses of an anxiety medicine.

He starts telling me about the spiders he sees everywhere in his hospital room. He picks at the empty air, saying he is trying to catch the little buggers. This is a type of delirium that is typical for alcoholic withdrawal. His blood tests go wild. The liver is failing dramatically, unable to clear ammonia from the blood. This causes further delirium and confusion. He develops encephalopathy and falls into a coma and dies after four days.

His death is a loss for the town. He was quite a character.

diabetes

Why is diabetes so common in the rural South?

A fair proportion of my practice involves treating patients with diabetes.

Cora Ellsworth is typical. She is 56 years old, and she used to drive a school bus. She is on disability now because she can hardly walk. She has terrible arthritis in her knees. She uses a walker to get around. She is overweight, like much of the community. She is 5'4" tall and weighs over 300 pounds. Her knees are shot because that much weight is hard on the knees. The joints give out from the wear and tear imposed on them.

She is a talker. She tells me with each visit about her children and grandchildren, whom she helps take care of. I see her frequently for her various medical complaints. She mostly talks about hoping to lose weight so the orthopedic surgeon will agree to give her knee replacements. My chief concern, though, is her diabetes.

Cora has Diabetes Type 2, as do a quarter of my patients. Her blood sugar stays high. Normally, the body regulates levels of blood sugar via the production of insulin from the pancreas. The insulin produced then finds its way to receptors on muscle cells and elsewhere, expediting the intake of glucose from the bloodstream.

The problem is the body no longer recognizes it.

In Type I diabetes—the kind that youngsters get—there is a failure of the pancreas to make insulin. The doctor provides a prescription for shots of insulin and voilà, the patients are better. At least until they turn into rebellious teenagers and start refusing to take their insulin as prescribed.

In Type 2 diabetes, the kind that middle-aged people get—especially those who are obese—the defect is not in the pancreas. Plenty of insulin is made. The problem is the body no longer recognizes it. The receptors on muscle cells and elsewhere have become insensitive to insulin. They do not see it. The glucose does NOT get moved into the body cells. Instead, it stays put in the bloodstream and wreaks havoc.

High blood sugar will cause damage throughout the body. It damages the retina and can cause blindness. It damages the kidneys and is a common cause of kidney failure. It damages the heart and is a common cause of heart disease.

There are treatments for Type 2 diabetes. Ms. Cora takes three different pills for diabetes, and her endocrinologist has recently started her on a fourth one. Her diabetes control remains marginal. Her glucose levels occasionally soar, but we can usually get them to something below the panic level.

Ms. Cora already has angina—chest pains due to heart disease. She sees a cardiologist for regular follow-up. She sees a nephrologist who keeps an eye on her kidney function.

I see Ms. Cora for follow-up every three months. She is still trying to lose weight. She has lost 20 pounds and will need to lose another 50 pounds before the orthopedic surgeon is willing to do knee replacements. I celebrate the weight loss with her. She keeps me up to date on the activities of the grandchildren. I monitor the list of medicines she is on. It is a long list, given the diabetes meds and the heart meds and the pain meds.

She keeps me up to date on the activities of the grandchildren.

I know, as her physician, that there is little I can do for her, other than trying to keep her stable on her assortment of meds.

the burden of diabetes on the community

I have seen twenty other patients like her; patients with difficult-to-treat diabetes. I have taken care of several in the hospital, as they struggle with end-stage renal disease or congestive heart failure.

Why is diabetes so common in the rural south? In large part, it is due to the genetics. It runs in families and the families who settled here apparently carried the genes for adult-onset diabetes with them. Diabetes is also related to the rate of obesity. The rural south has more obesity than other regions of the country.

This may be due to the foods that are eaten in this region. Recipes often include bacon and mayonnaise. Chicken is deep fried. There is no premium placed on eating fresh fruit and vegetables. I do not know if this reflects poverty and buying foods that cost less, or from family recipes passed down for generations. The net result, however, is the same. Many people are overweight.

Local Color

more on law enforcement in town

tall pete

Pete is a tall policeman in town. He towers over everyone at 6'5".

He told me this story in the clinic. He says he had gone to the bank to take care of private business. He was getting back into his personal truck in the parking lot. From the perch of his seat in his truck, he watched as two men pulled up alongside him and started unloading shotguns from the trunk of their car.

He said he had an excellent view of what they were doing. They were heading toward the back entrance of the bank. He climbed down from his truck, identified himself as police, and arrested them.

Clearly, these would-be robbers were from out of town. Everyone in town knew what Pete looked like and what his truck looked like. This bank was located across the street from the high school. This was a red-letter day for the town. The school went on shutdown, given the activity nearby. The high school kids were thrilled. Rx

Local Color

pancake

There was also the time a young woman in town hired a young man named "Pancake" to help move her single-wide trailer from one mobile home park to another.

Pancake was a good old boy from town. He had never been the sharpest tool in the shed, according to local lore. He borrowed a tractor from a friend and started pulling the trailer down the highway that ran past the town. The tractor broke down. The trailer was stuck on the side of what turned out to be a state highway. The sheriff was called. He was obligated to push the trailer off the highway because it is illegal to block a state highway. The trailer was severely damaged as it got pushed into the ditch alongside the road.

This story attracted the attention of the national news services. Everyone felt sorry for the lady who owned the trailer. Heck, she and her two kids and their dogs were inside the trailer as Pancake was moving it, it was supposed to be only a short trip up the road.

The sheriff in town got roundly castigated by folk as far away as California for being mean to the owner of the trailer. People from around the country sent in donations to the young woman so she could buy a new trailer. She got $30,000, to everyone's amazement, and she bought an upgrade—a doublewide trailer.

There were T-shirts one could buy on the internet, saying: "Never hire someone named Pancake to move your doublewide." Now the status gap between a single and doublewide trailer is enormous, but the creators of the T-shirt apparently were unaware of the distinction.

what I learned:

To appreciate police officers and firemen.
They were part of the Emergency Room landscape,
almost part of the staff. They were genuinely concerned for the
welfare of citizenry and of the patients who came our way.
I also learned that malfeasance can sometimes be amusing.

CHAPTER FIFTEEN

on death and dying

What better gift to their mother—
their love and company as she quietly passed into a final sleep.

My patients taught me lots of things.

- ✓ They certainly taught me what death looks like. It was reassuring in a way.

- ✓ They taught me that the best deaths are when you have family and friends nearby. And this small town did insist on close families. In the hospital or the nursing home, there were always family and friends nearby.

- ✓ They took visiting hours seriously. Four or five relatives would show up nightly, to visit a parent or grandparent.

the good death

The patient in room three of the little rural hospital where I worked was 84 and dying of kidney failure. The excess potassium, sodium, and protein in her blood were no longer being filtered by her kidneys. Instead of being excreted in her urine, they were building up in her bloodstream.

She slept much of the day and when awake, she was less aware of her surroundings.

Her two daughters had come to keep her company. They were decidedly middle-aged women, well into their fifties. They moved into her hospital room. Each had a cot, supplied by the nurses. They took their meals in the room, again supplied by the nurses.

They told stories of their shared childhood. Every day I came to the hospital to do rounds. Every day I stopped into their mother's room, the two sisters were telling stories of adventures they had had as children. They would talk to their mom, ask if she remembered this or that: the time the younger one had wandered into the barn and fallen asleep and they couldn't find her for hours; or the time they went sledding and one of them broke her leg.

"Yes, I remember," the mother would answer.

As the days went on, the stories continued but the mom would answer less often. She passed into a comalike state. She died after three days, still with her daughters keeping her company. They loved her. What better gift to their mother—their love and company as she quietly passed into a final sleep.

what this taught me:

I have seen other patients die. One 76-year-old man was a rather simple guy who had worked as a farmer his whole life. He had never gone past ninth grade in school. He told me he was seeing his mother in his hospital room as he lay dying of lung disease. He would be talking to her as I entered the room.

He had never meet his mother. His mother had died when he was born. He said he was looking forward to seeing her in heaven. I knew this because he was related to my office manager, who

> *told me as much. Everyone was related to everyone else in this little town. But this man nonetheless had a full visualization of what she looked like. He found comfort in the knowledge that she would welcome him in the hereafter. He was not afraid.*
>
> *I have seen the anticipation of rejoining loved ones in the here after with other patients. I believe it is a comfort that God provides for us as we make the transition from life to death.*

road warrior

Mr. Johnson is a retired military man. This is evident in the way he holds himself erect, with precise movements. Pushing age 70, he is still handsome and fit.

At first I see him in the clinic for the usual: blood pressure medicines, cholesterol medicines. Then, after a few years, he starts complaining of getting short of breath with minimal exertion. He takes a daily seven-mile walk around the lake where he and his wife live. He tells me he is unable to walk the seven miles. He is getting winded halfway through.

He goes to the VA and sees a lung specialist. He is diagnosed with lung disease: "smoker's lung." This is not altogether unexpected, as he has spent forty years smoking two packs a day.

He sets out on his cross-country journey.

A year passes. He is now wearing portable oxygen on his walks around the lake. As his lung disease progresses, the oxygen flow rate is bumped up from the standard two liters per minute to three liters per minute. The need for that high a flow rate is not a good sign. He understands from his VA doctor that his lungs are getting worse, and that he is heading into significant disability and a sedentary lifestyle soon. Being bound to an oxygen tank and confined to his living room is not appealing.

So, what does he do? He decides to ride his motorcycle across the country with his 40-year-old son as a travel companion. He packs his oxygen tank into the saddle bag. Nasal canula in place, feeding oxygen to his lungs, he sets out on his cross-country journey. He is starting in Kentucky and heading west to California.

His wife is also a patient of mine. She is not happy with his departure on his motorcycle. She keeps me posted on his progress across the country.

Three weeks into his trip, he makes it as far as Santa Fe, New Mexico. The altitude in Santa Fe is 7,000 feet above sea level. If one is already on supplemental oxygen, one will need even more to compensate for the thin air. His wife tells me his oxygen tank ran out. He died alongside the road he loved on the outskirts of Santa Fe. She is in tears as she tells me this.

I could understand his impulse to go on one more road trip. He understood he was dying and wanted to do it in a burst of glory, like the warrior he was.

what this patient taught me:

People approach death differently. Many choose withdrawal to the comfort of home and family. Some choose to have one last adventure. The image of him on his motorcycle traveling cross-country—especially to the southwest, with its glorious open spaces—makes me want to applaud the decision he made. However, that was cold comfort for the wife who was left behind.

And yes, the son made it back safely.

I have already mentioned that many folk in Kentucky are evangelicals and southern Baptists. They do not believe in evolution. They are firm believers in a literal interpretation of the Bible. They are also firm believers in going to hell if you sin and fail to repent.

the lady who was burning in hell

I was making rounds in the little rural hospital where I work. The nurses are generally good, and they are experienced. Most of them had been working for twenty years or more. One of the nurses tells me, when I arrive at the nurses' station, that the patient in room five is upset. She says she feels like she is on fire. She believes she is burning in hell, the nurse tells me.

I review her chart. The patient is 76 years old. She was admitted with end-stage kidney disease. She is under the care of hospice. Her kidneys are failing.

I go to see the patient. She is slender and pale. She looks older than 76 because her color is poor. She is restless in bed.

"My skin is burning up," she says. "I am going to hell."

I do not know this patient very well. She was admitted by another doctor. But I understand, from what she is saying, that she is deeply religious. She prays to Jesus. I have nothing left in my doctor bag of tricks. There are no medicines I can give her. She is already on everything we could think of to handle anxiety or pain.

I sit down next to her bed. I find a copy of the New Testament in the bed stand. I open the Bible to the Gospels and read to her. I try to comfort her. I touch her hand at times. She calms down a little.

She finally falls asleep, which is all I could ask for as a doctor.

I turn to the Psalms that I know better than the Gospels. "The Lord is my Shepherd, I shall not want," I read to her from Psalm 23.

I try to find words of comfort. Some of the Psalms are unduly upsetting, with too much emphasis on "I will slay my enemies." I scan ahead and keep it to words of comfort. She finally falls asleep, which is all I could ask for as a doctor.

I suspect the sensation of burning in hell stems from the kidney disease. The buildup of toxins in the bloodstream can cause discomfort and an altered sensation in the skin. As for the insistence that she deserves to go to hell, I do not know what secret shame or sin she holds onto at the hospital.

I tell her repeatedly that I do not believe that God wants her to burn in hell. This is easy for me to say; I do not believe in hell.

The nurse on staff knows I was reading the New Testament to her. She thinks this is genuinely nice of me. I do not know if she is aware that I am Jewish. Considering this, it is even nicer of me.

The patient dies overnight. May she rest in peace.

Local Color
more on religion in the south

I hire a young woman, Cindy Dennis, to work in the clinic. She is in her late twenties and recently graduated from a training program that is part of a Southern Baptist-sponsored college. I did not pay much attention to the locale of her training, but I should have. Her fundamentalist training leads to some awkward situations.

The first arises early on in her employment. Cindy sees patients by herself in the exam room, makes a diagnosis, and writes an appropriate medicine. Sandra Harris, a patient of mine, tells me that Cindy had seen her the previous week. Sandra tells me, with some distress, that Cindy dropped to her knees and prayed for Sandra.

This was especially distressing to Sandra because she had come in for treatment of a sinus infection. Cindy's posture on her knees and her prayers to God led Sandra to believe that she was dying.

I ask Cindy to refrain from praying in front of patients, unless the patient requests it, of course.

Other awkward situations arose as well. She continues to proffer (unasked) opinions about birth control and declare how it is against God's law. I eventually take Cindy aside and explain to her the boundaries between faith and medicine.

Cindy left after one year. The next physician assistant we hired was someone with more clinical experience and common sense who graduated from a publicly-funded training program.

CHAPTER SIXTEEN

fainting: common and uncommon reasons

Your brain loses its supply of blood and out you go.

People come in all the time complaining of "fainting." This always gives me pause. I pray that the next words out of their mouth will be: "I got dizzy, the room started spinning." If they sat down and felt better within a minute or two, then I can pronounce a diagnosis, "Aha! Vertigo! I can give you a medicine that will help." I can reassure them that this is a common complaint and is usually transient. They should be better in another week or so.

So ... let us say there was no spinning. Perhaps they got light-headed and slipped gently to the ground. Perhaps this was when something scared them, or they got upset for some reason. Perhaps they came to within a minute or so.

Still excellent if they answer yes to the above prompts. If this is a rare event and usually triggered by something stressful, then the diagnosis is still at hand: "Vasovagal syncope." A fancy name for the common faint.

This happened to me once. It probably has happened at some point to most people. For me, my ex-husband called to tell me that the car he was supposed to give me had died on the highway and was inoperable. I felt faint and slid to the floor, phone still grasped in my hand. This was back in the day when phones were connected to the wall by a cord.

The mechanism has to do with stimulation of the vagus nerve, triggered by an overwhelming stress, no doubt with an underlying ancient reflex arc at play. The stimulation of the vagus nerve causes your blood pressure to plummet. Your brain loses its supply of blood and out you go. When you are prone on the floor, the hydrodynamics of blood flow get rectified, and you get back to your feet but just don't do it too quickly.

What if the situation is more complicated? What if the patient says "no" to every one of your questions regarding spinning or antecedent stress?

Then the diagnostic endeavor becomes more challenging.

The following two vignettes describe patients with complaints of "I keep fainting." Each taught me something of the complexity of the diagnosis and treatment for this seemingly simple complaint.

the girl who kept fainting

Mrs. Tuttle and her daughter Andrea are in the clinic. Andrea is 15 and clearly does not want to be here. The mother has dragged her in to see a doctor because the school nurse keeps calling and telling her, "Come pick up your daughter! She has fainted again."

Mrs. Tuttle does most of the talking. The young girl is not talkative. I nonetheless try to draw her out. I need her input. Is there something that makes her faint? Has she skipped breakfast or lunch?

None of these pertain. Andrea says it happens at random times. "When I'm standing during choir practice, I get hot and lightheaded. I've fainted twice at choir practice. I've fainted other places, too." She describes sliding quietly to the floor, landing in a heap. She doesn't get hurt when she falls. She comes to within two to three minutes.

Other than being enormously embarrassed by fainting, the young girl would otherwise be okay.

Andrea is sent to the lab to have blood drawn. While she is out of the room, the mom tells me she has been worried about her for a while. Andrea has just started high school and seems overwhelmed, according to her mother. She is having trouble making friends. She is becoming increasingly phobic about social situations.

The school wanted a thorough checkup. I sent her to the pediatric neurologist, Dr. Tisch. He put her through a battery of tests. This took a full day. I saw Mrs. Tuttle shortly thereafter, for follow-up. She tells me how traumatizing the day had been: "Dr. Tisch was

He just has no patience with those patients who have less deadly diagnoses.

angry with Andrea for wasting his time! That's what he said. He said the tests were all negative. He told her there was nothing wrong with her. That it was all in her head."

The mom tells me Andrea started crying after he spoke to her like that. I sent Mrs. Tuttle home shortly thereafter and called my doctor friend Lauren. She herself was conversant with psychiatric disorders. She was a virtual treasure trove of knowledge regarding mental illness and its variants.

"It's called conversion disorder," Lauren told me. "When someone is anxious, these feelings can be translated into physical symptoms. This young girl faints. Someone else might have a different manifestation, but it's still due to the underlying anxiety or stress."

This was helpful, a nice simple diagnosis. I referred Andrea to a therapist. She was started on medicines for anxiety and depression. She got better.

I have since seen other patients with uncontrollable shaking of the extremities or other physical symptoms; others whom a neurologist had declared free of seizure disorder or any kind of brain lesion. Not all neurologists are as disagreeable as Dr. Tisch. I know he is an excellent doctor for those patients who DO have seizures or DO have brain lesions. He just has no patience with those patients who have less deadly diagnoses.

buying time

Lisa Maddox is a young woman in her early forties. She is married, with two half-grown children. She and her husband own a farm. They grow tobacco and keep cattle. She is well-groomed, with a pleasant oval face and brown hair. I have known her for some time. Mostly, she tells me how she is doing with her sugar levels. She was diagnosed with Type 1 diabetes as a child and has been on insulin shots ever since.

By and large she has been doing well, considering how deadly the diagnosis of childhood diabetes used to be. She came through two pregnancies. Her diabetes specialist is good, and she has been diligent about keeping to her schedule of finger sticks and insulin injections.

This time, she is complaining of dizziness. "Every time I stand up, I get lightheaded. I almost faint." In fact, she says she has fainted a few times.

Mrs. Mattox says the dizziness has been going on for the last two weeks and is getting worse. In the clinic, we check her blood pressure. It is normal when she is sitting down. We then check it when she stands up. It plummets! No wonder she is fainting. It takes a fair amount of blood pressure to push blood up to the brain. If it is too low, the brain complains by shutting down. She gets dizzy in the clinic. We have her sit down again.

After a few minutes, the lightheadedness passes.

She slowly recovers. After a few minutes, the lightheadedness passes. This looks like autonomic neuropathy. I consult with my neurologist friend up the street. She recommends starting the patient on medicines to regulate her blood pressure, to keep it from bottoming out and to give her extra salt in her diet. And it's another way to keep blood pressure higher than it would be otherwise.

I see her for follow-up in the clinic one week later. She is doing better. She is taking her daily medicine and getting through the day without fainting. She is also trying to change position slowly, to avoid standing up too quickly.

Autonomic neuropathy is not a good sign. It means that she has ongoing damage to her nervous system. Specifically, the nervous system that is in charge of regulating blood pressure and heart rate. Two rather critical functions.

As for so many things, diabetes is the usual culprit. The high blood sugar plays havoc with the nerve fibers that run through the body. Over time, the damage builds up and the nerves no longer work.

There is no cure for this level of nerve damage. We can treat the specific complaint of getting dizzy when she stands up, but we are only buying her time. The other disorders to expect, such as problems with her stomach and with her heart, we will not be able to treat so easily.

Personal aside: I am writing this during the COVID-19 pandemic. As I have gotten older—and as we continue to shelter in place during this difficult time—my outlook on disease and death has changed. In the final analysis, all any of us can ask for is more time. My standard for medical intervention used to be "restoration of good health" or "cure." Now, I consider "buying more time" an acceptable goal.

The autonomic nervous system consists of two parts. The sympathetic nervous system runs on adrenalin. It's the nervous system that gets you all fired up when confronted by danger, providing the fight or flight response. The heart begins to race, and the adrenalin provides the burst of energy that enables one to flee from a saber-toothed tiger (in caveman times) or to respond to getting cut off in traffic (in modern times).

The *parasympathetic nervous system,* on the other hand, is in charge of settling us down again, after a surge of adrenalin. Once we are back in the safety of our cave and no longer in danger, it allows us to relax. It tamps down the racing heart and brings it back to a sedate rhythm; it enables us to enjoy a meal and to digest it; it promotes sexual arousal— something else besides eating that we and our caveman forebears could enjoy once safely back home.

The second nervous system provides a control mechanism for the first one. If the saber-toothed tiger got us all riled up in the afternoon, the second circuit settles down all systems and allows us to relax at night.

The only time when doctors pay any mind to the dance between these two nervous systems is when it is out of kilter. Again, this is mostly in patients with long-standing diabetes. This degree of nerve damage is not that common. It is never a good sign.

Local Color
the wonders of synthroid
and the silver-tongued doctor

Patricia Snoop is a new patient in the clinic. She is 38 years old. Her chief complaint is "not wanting to have sex," at least according to her husband, who is speaking on her behalf, as he is lurking on a chair in the corner. He is a mechanic and wearing grease-spattered work clothes and heavy work boots.

On exam, she looks markedly older than 38. Her skin is puffy and coarse. She is overweight and slow of speech.

Upon further questioning, it turns out she used to be on Synthroid. This is proffered by the husband. The patient herself is a woman of few words.

She took Synthroid last year after being diagnosed with a low thyroid hormone. Synthroid is a synthetic version of the thyroid hormone that her body was apparently no longer making. The formal diagnosis would be "hypothyroidism," which means (in doctor language) "low thyroid."

The husband tells me, "She felt better after six months on the medicine, so she quit using it."

I ask more questions related to signs and symptoms of hypothyroidism. She has gained a lot of weight in the interim, her periods have disappeared, and she is tired all the time. None of these other complaints seemed to bother the husband. The only one that really got to him was that she had no interest in sex.

This got his interest.

Now, these are all classic signs of dangerously low levels of thyroid hormone. I told the two of them that she needed to go back on the medicine and to stay on it for the rest of her life.

The husband wasn't sure she needed it. I patiently explained, "She won't want to have sex unless she stays on Synthroid!"

This got his interest. She restarted Synthroid.

I saw her for a follow-up visit four weeks later. She was a new woman. She was bright, talkative, and slender. She looked ten years younger, and the husband was happy.

what this taught me:
Know your audience. The intricacies of hypothyroidism
and the fact that it can kill you if untreated
did not grab the husband's attention. The lack of sex did.
You have to go with whatever hook you can.

challenging situations

Make sure everyone is sitting down
when you have one of these life-and-death family conferences.

There are patient encounters which are challenging and thus unforgettable. Challenging situations arise in different flavors. There is the one that asks me to be a counselor and spiritual support and doctor all at the same time, when dealing with a clan of family members concerned about a diagnosis of cancer in the *paterfamilias*.

There is the one where a young man is looking extremely sick with no obvious diagnosis dancing in my head. This calls for an admission of "I don't know," and the quick referral to the ER.

A third instance involves a sick gman with multiple health risks whose right-sided abdominal pain has eluded diagnosis thus far. All three situations cause a spike in the doctor's levels of stress hormones. Each taught me a lesson, however painful.

the family conference

I knew Eddie Claiborne well. Occasionally, I see his wife more frequently as a patient because she comes to the clinic for treatment of anxiety and depression. Eddie is usually the strong, silent type who keeps her company at appointments. He is around 50 years old and makes a living as a farmer.

I know that he has an older brother who had died of pancreatic cancer. I know Eddie recently headed up the road to Big City Hospital with a complaint of searing abdominal pain. He spent a week getting poked at, and imaged, and biopsied. He left with a diagnosis of pancreatic cancer. It is not supposed to run in families but, there you have it: it apparently does ... at least in his family.

He and his wife are in the clinic this afternoon to ask me questions about what to expect regarding this devastating diagnosis.

I am not looking forward to this visit. What could I possibly tell them? My preliminary impression of pancreatic cancer is that it kills you quickly. I suspect the average survival time is only two to six months after diagnosis.

I express my sympathy at the predicament the family faces.

I look it up in the medical texts and online medical reports. I see nothing in my reading that changes my understanding of how deadly this cancer is for anyone. Steve Jobs, the brilliant founder of Apple computer, died of the same disease not long before this time.

When I enter the exam room, this is what I see: Eddie Claiborne sitting down, looking a little worse for wear after his hospitalization. He appears perhaps a bit pale and a bit gaunt. He otherwise remains quiet and stoic. His wife—a slender woman, a bit frenetic—is standing next to him. Their sons and daughters-in-law are also in the room, and it is a full house.

I try to draw upon whatever reserves of strength I possess. I try to draw myself up to my full height. Not so easy, since height-wise, I am only 5'2" tall. I express my sympathy at the predicament the family faces.

"I am so sorry to hear of your illness," I say. "I know your brother had the same diagnosis. I know you have questions to ask. I'll try my best to answer them. Although I am sure your doctors at Big City Hospital already gave you some idea of what to expect ... what treatments and what options there are."

"The doctors said they could give him pain medicines," the wife says. "They said there wasn't much more they could do. Is that right? There must be something!"

There is an awkward silence for a minute.

"I am afraid that is true," I say. "There are no medicines or chemo or radiation that make a significant difference. Pancreatic cancer is difficult to treat."

"How long? How long does he have?" the wife says. She is close to tears as she pleads with me. The sons and daughters-in-law stand close to her. They are trying to be supportive.

I have no recourse but to tell the truth.

"From what I can tell from the research I've done, it just corroborates what your doctors at the Big City Hospital said. There is nothing they can do other than pain meds," I say as gently as possible. "People with a diagnosis of pancreatic cancer live only about two months or maybe four more months before they die. I am so sorry."

At this point, the wife faints.

I am not expecting that particular response. The wife is helped to her feet by the nearest daughter-in-law. The wife is shaky but ambulatory. Eddie Claiborne is still quiet and stoic.

"Thank you, Dr. T," Eddie says. "I sort of knew what to expect after what happened to my brother. It's better to know what the score is."

"I am so sorry, Mr. Claiborne," I say. "Let me know how things go. If you need me, I'll be here. Otherwise, I would trust the doctors at the Big City Hospital. They are doing the best anyone can."

The family leaves. I never forget the wife who faints. Eddie Claiborne dies three months later.

The wife collapses emotionally at the time of his death. They had been married for thirty years and she is lost. But she comes through the tragedy. After a year or two, she starts looking less empty and starts picking up the pieces of her life. Despite her apparent frailty, she is a survivor.

Postscript. This happened years ago. In the interim, family clusters of pancreatic cancer have been reported. It is rare but not unknown.

The doctors in the city had already told them of the dismal prognosis for pancreatic cancer. They had already researched the topic and already knew what to expect. This conference in the little exam room was a kind of ritual—a ritual for them to hear the words again. The husband certainly understood. He had already watched his brother die about one year earlier.

The other thing this conference taught me: make sure everyone is sitting down when you have one of these life-and-death family conferences.

the handsome pakistani doctor reappears

There are patients you can help: see them through a crisis, give them a magic medicine that makes everything better. There are others where there is little you can do. Their distress is beyond cure. The following story is about one person I could help. Plus, the handsome Pakistani surgeon reappears, at least in spirit if not in person.

Tony Bowman is a man in his early 50s. I see him fairly often in the clinic, mostly for follow-ups for his diabetes. He has type 2 diabetes. He has done reasonably well on oral medicines and a daily injection of insulin.

I sometimes wonder if he comes in so frequently to socialize. Some patients like to talk. He mostly tells me about his social life. There is ongoing drama about an ex-girlfriend and his pursuit of a new girlfriend. There is some discussion of Viagra, as his romantic life needs a tweak. On the latter topic, I tell him to check with his cardiologist first for safety reasons. He is indeed cleared for its use and his social life improves afterward.

Tony had a heart attack two years before. He had bypass surgery that involve splitting open his chest. The surgery had gone fine, but he had some problems afterward when the surgical wound got infected. He was in the hospital for another month on strong antibiotics with a Staph infection (MRSA) that was resistant to the usual antibiotics. This won him another specialist: the infectious disease doctor. He has been monitored since then for any further recurrence of MRSA. He has done well until now.

This time when I see him in the clinic, he is obviously in pain. He s clutching the right side of his stomach. He is pale and running a fever of 101. He tells me the pain started two weeks ago and has come and gone since then. He has been to the ER twice with his pain. Both times, he had tests done to rule out gallbladder disease, the usual cause for right sided abdominal pain. The tests were negative. He was sent home on antibiotics and pain medicines. He hasn't gotten any better.

I remember another patient I had seen with type 2 diabetes who also had right sided abdominal pain. His tests for gallbladder disease had also been negative. His symptoms had also gotten worse, with disabling pain and fever, until finally the handsome Pakistani surgeon —let us call him "Dr. Mo"—decided to do an exploratory surgery. That meant taking a look at the gallbladder and abdomen to see what he could see. He saw plenty.

The surgery was done across the hall from where I was seeing my hospital patients that day. The surgical staff told me about finding a gallbladder that was infected, swollen to the point that it was rupturing and spilling its contents into the abdominal cavity. The surgical team had to move quickly and scramble in the operating room to excise the gallbladder and to wash out the surrounding areas. The surgery made for a dramatic retelling.

Tests in that case confirmed MRSA infection. After the surgery, the patient got potent antibiotics—stronger than the ones he had already been on—and survived.

With this case in mind, I send Tony back to the Emergency Room, speaking to the ER doctor after he has had a chance to evaluate the patient. The ER doctor tells me he had had another ultrasound and other test, to again check for gallstones. The tests were again negative. To my distress, the ER doctor is about to send Tony home again.

Tony did have a raging infection in his gall-bladder. He was close to sepsis.

I tell the doctor about this other patient I had seen, some years before, with a gallbladder that was rupturing by the time he made it to surgery. The young doctor on the other end of the phone agreed to have the surgeon on call look at the patient. Tony went to surgery later that evening.

I talked to the hospital staff in the morning to discover that Tony did have a raging infection in his gallbladder, that he was close to sepsis, which is deadly. This was MRSA again. He needed a prolonged course of IV antibiotics that would target MRSA. The surgery had saved his life.

One of the advantages of experience is that I'd heard a similar case before and paid attention to Tony's symptoms. Plus, the previous case had been unforgettable: the drama in the Operating Room and the skilled hands of the handsome Dr. Mo.

Tony spent a month in the hospital before making a full recovery. He continued seeing me in the clinic with further stories of his romantic entanglements.

On a separate, largely unrelated note, I remember a young woman I worked with in the ER. She was a pretty, young person—no more than 23. She was funny. One time she said, "I think Dr. Mo is awfully handsome. He can do surgery on me anytime he wants to … ." I think this was a sexual innuendo. She did not need any surgery.

puzzle pieces

Doctors like to solve puzzles. These are ideally diagnostic puzzles. Although, in down times, crossword puzzles or picture puzzles will do in a pinch. The following is a story about a patient whose illness was unsolvable: the pieces of the puzzle did not fit together. No matter how you tried to force a diagnosis out of the disparate pieces of data, it did not feel right. Sometimes the best you can do is to say, "I do not know why you are sick." This is always a hard thing to say to a patient because it lessens your sheen as an all-knowing and infallible physician. But it is honest and does lead to other paths that ideally will enable someone—if not you—to solve the puzzle.

Richard Spencer is a 27-year-old man who is a new patient in the clinic. Like so many young men, he is usually healthy and has no reason to see the inside of a doctor's office. This time, however, his girlfriend has dragged him in. She is worried about him.

He looks pale and bedraggled: hair uncombed; clothes rumpled; and hands shaking. He tells me he works as a cook in a restaurant. He hasn't felt well for at least a week. The story emerges in bits and pieces. He is not a talkative guy.

"How long have you been sick?" I ask.

"Dunno. Maybe a week. Not really sick, just don't feel well."

"Any fevers?" I ask.

"Maybe at the beginning, for a couple of days. I don't have a thermometer."

"Anyone else sick at home or at work?" I ask.

"Not that I know of."

"Are you having pain anywhere?" I ask.

"No, not really."

"Are you able to eat and drink okay?" I ask.

"No, not really hungry."

None of these answers are particularly alarming. He could have a viral infection which will resolve on its own. I review his vital signs.

His temperature is low-normal. His blood pressure is low-normal. And then I get to his heartrate: 120 beats per minute! A normal heartrate is 70. There is no known universe where a heartrate like that lives alongside such vague complaints.

The physical exam is likewise a puzzle. It is normal except for the racing heart and the obvious shakiness of his hands.

I ask him to get a chest X-ray, which could show pneumonia in the lungs. I notice as he goes down the hall to the X-ray room how unsteady he is on his feet. I worry he may need help, although it is a short distance. He manages to get there and back on his own. The chest X-ray is normal.

Labs are drawn. By and large they too are normal. No evidence of anemia. No evidence of liver or kidney infection. I am at a diagnostic dead end. I cannot name what is wrong with him. I had been hoping that something would emerge from the medley of tests.

All I know for sure is that he does not look right. His heartrate makes no sense, not in tandem with his other vital signs. His unsteadiness of gait makes no sense either. Whatever is wrong with him, it is worrisome.

I tell him I do not know what is making him feel bad. I ask him to go to the emergency room. I tell him and his girlfriend that he needs to directly to the ER because it could be something serious.

I am trying not to say "Something serious, like impending death," but that is what I am thinking. He is not fully engaged in the clinic. He is somewhere in dreamland. His girlfriend, however, promises to take him directly to the ER.

I give them a 30 minute head start and then I call the ER to make sure they got there. I have had a few patients who get lost or lose interest en route, even after promising me they will go.

After another two hours, I call the ER back and ask how he's doing. The ER reports that he is in sepsis! He is going to be admitted. I am glad they have a diagnosis. Sepsis means he has a raging infection of some kind, such that body systems are shutting down. A bacterial or viral infection can trigger an out-of-control immune response. The immune system attacks the blood vessels and causes a low blood pressure. It somehow triggers a rapid heartrate as well. The net result can be organ failure and death. The kidneys shut down for lack of blood supply, and the brain goes off-system for the same reason.

He is kept in the hospital for a week. He needs intravenous fluids to support his blood pressure. He needs strong antibiotics to treat what turns out to be appendicitis. When I see him for follow-up, he looks like a new man. His color is good, his hair is combed, and he is wearing clean clothes. His hands are no longer shaking. His speech is fluent. So, it is a happy outcome.

More on Sepsis

Sepsis can be deadly. The out-of-control immune response —with blood pressure in the basement, with organ failure— is thought to have been the cause of millions of deaths in the 1918 flu epidemic. I am writing this in 2020. We are now experiencing the COVID-19 pandemic. In hospitalized patients with COVID-19, sepsis is not an uncommon cause of death, especially in younger patients. We now call a raging immune response *cytokine storm*. We throw steroids at it, with some success at shutting it down. There is still a lot we do not know. In the final analysis, sepsis is still a daunting diagnosis.

CHAPTER EIGHTEEN

nature of doctoring

*Support and strengthen me in my task
so that I may aid those in need.*

Even after working as a doctor for two decades, I continue to hone my skills. As described in the following chapter, I discover it helps me to say a prayer before starting the day; I develop an intuitive sense of when a patient is seriously ill; and I learn to respect Dr. Death. There is also an essay thrown in on the history of the erstwhile symbol of medicine, the caduceus—the winged rod with two entwined snakes.

the prayer of maimonides

Every morning I would drive through horse farms and rural country side to get to work. As I drove, I would wonder what patient or what dilemma I would be facing that day in the clinic. I would say a prayer:

*God, give me strength. Give me patience.
Give me the wisdom to treat my patients as they need to be treated.*

I needed to say that prayer. Without it, I was not sure I would have the strength, patience, or wisdom I needed for what my day might bring. Doctoring requires all three.

Patients can suck the strength from me. They try to wheedle and cajole and get pain meds from me to feed an addiction.

They try my patience. When I ask, "When did you first start coughing?" they start telling me a long story about going to visit their great-uncle in Tennessee and how everyone there was sick with a stomach bug. But this does not answer my question of when their cough started.

They make demands on my store of wisdom. Their chief complaint might be: "I have a rash," but what they are sick from is more serious, like rheumatoid arthritis.

I stole this prayer directly from the colorful framed graphic I have hanging in the office, the Prayer of Maimonides. It cheered me up to look at it throughout my busy days.

O Benevolent God. Thou hast created the human being with infinite wisdom. Thou hast blessed Thine earth, Thy mountains, and Thy rivers with healing substances that enable Thy children to alleviate their sufferings and to heal their illnesses. Thou hast chosen me to keep vigil over the life and well-being of Thy creations.

Purify me, and fill my heart with love, for my art and for Thy creations. Endow me with strength of mind and heart, so that both be always ready to serve all that need me, be they rich or poor, good, or wicked, friend or foe. Let me never see in the sufferer anything else but a fellow human being in pain.

Grant me perseverance to continually expand my knowledge, for wisdom is boundless and can extend infinitely to enrich the human mind with new discoveries.

O compassionate God, Thou hast chosen me to watch over
the health of Thy creation. I now apply myself to my calling.
Support and strengthen me in my task so that I may aid
those in need.

—*Maimonides' Prayer for the Physician, 1200 AD*

Maimonides was born in Cordoba in southern Spain in 1135
AD or so. The Moors controlled the country. They were blacks from
North Africa, Islamic in religion. They were tolerant of the Jews and
Christians who lived alongside them.

The Moors were part of the greater Arab world, which at that
time was at the cutting edge of scientific and medical knowledge.
The Arabs had translated the ancient Greek manuscripts into Arabic.
Thus, Maimonides studied medicine at schools that taught the works
of Hippocrates, Aristotle, and Galen. It would be another 400 years
until the rest of Europe and
the West "rediscovered" the
ancient Greek store of medical knowledge.

**I find the Prayer of Maimonides
more helpful than the alternative,
the famous Oath of Hippocrates.**

Some years later, the town
of Cordoba was taken over by a different faction of Moslems. This
new group was markedly less tolerant of their Jewish and Christian
neighbors. The conquerors forced the non-Moslems to leave.
Maimonides and his young family fled Cordoba and sought refuge
in Morocco and then Egypt.

Maimonides continued his medical practice in Egypt. He was such
an excellent physician that the great Saladin hired him for his court.

I find the Prayer of Maimonides more helpful than the alternative, the famous Oath of Hippocrates written by the famous Greek
physician around 400 BC, centuries before Maimonides' prayer.

Medical students are often required to recite an edited version of
the Hippocratic Oath when they graduate. Its most famous excerpt:
"First, do no harm." This is excellent advice for any would-be physician,

although it is unclear if it was included in the original iteration of the Oath.

Much of Hippocrates' Oath contains excellent advice. It sets ethical standards for physicians: "Be respectful to the physician who taught you; help the sick to the best of your ability; avoid sexual relations with those whose houses you visit; maintain confidentiality."

It does not address, however, the struggles of day-to-day doctoring.

Chief among these struggles is the need to fix your courage to the sticking point when confronting patients who may be manipulative, lying, or dying. Neither does it provide a path through a maze of possible diagnoses to find the one that works and best explains a medley of symptoms. For these dilemmas, I invoke Maimonides' prayer for patience, courage, and wisdom. And I breathe deeply.

oracle / physician
In her altered state, the words of Apollo
would issue forth from her mouth.

Some parts of doctoring are rewarding. When I examine a patient in distress and can actually name what is wrong with him or her, and maybe even fix it, that makes me feel awesome. When I arrive at the point where I can name a likely diagnosis, I feel like the oracle of ancient Greece. I am a seer and can speak a truth.

This is after I collect the history of the patient's illness; after I do a physical exam; and after I send off for labs or other tests. I also regularly dip into the medical books and lore that I have studied for twenty years. From the data and the research, I construct a likely diagnosis. It is almost entirely an intellectual exercise for me as the physician. It is a puzzle to be solved. Yes, there are emotional components in my interaction with the patient. I try to tread gently on his or her fears and feelings. But my responsibility is the conveyance of truth, where my judgment and the exam and tests lead me.

In the stories from ancient Greece, the Oracle served as a priestess of Apollo. The Oracle would sit in a chamber deep in the hillside of Delphi. She would inhale fumes that arose from a fissure in the earth. The fumes would induce a trance. In her altered state, the words of Apollo would issue forth from her mouth.

I feel like an oracle at times. When a patient presents with a series of complex symptoms that are puzzling at first, but then as the interview or the exam proceeds, I can see the image of "diagnosis X." It is not entirely an intellectual exercise at that point. Instead, it becomes an overwhelming sense of worry or fear with the name of some dire disease suddenly appearing in the ether above his or her head. These gut-level responses on my part are invariably correct. The Emergency Room or Imaging Center to which a person is sent confirms my diagnosis.

For example, a Canadian man appears in the clinic with a mysterious illness. He is 68 years old and grumbles that he "doesn't like doctors."

He also does not have insurance because he is from Canada. He does not understand the complex US system of medical care. He is used to easier access to health care than what we have in the US—not to mention free.

He is a reasonably slender gray-haired man who is well-spoken. He is complaining of hurting badly all over and especially in his back. He

The prognosis is not good.

says it started the day before. He thinks it is from going hiking two days before. When I ask him to lie down on the exam table, he shows ample evidence of pain. He moves with significant difficulty due to severe back pain. He complains of a swollen knot appearing over the right side of his groin.

On exam, I see a large mass the size of a tennis ball. He says this knot comes and goes. Today it has been staying and is painful. Something about his presentation and level of pain and mysterious mass reminds me of another patient, another man in his late sixties with a complaint of swelling in his abdomen and mysterious pain.

This other patient ended up with a diagnosis of lymphoma and metastatic cancer.

I send the Canadian to an imaging center for a CT scan of his back and abdomen. It comes back with a reading of prostate cancer that has metastasized. His back pain is due to the invasion of cancer into the vertebrae. The prognosis is not good.

The point being: the amount of pain he was in transported me to another time and place when another patient presented with a mystery pain and turned out to have metastatic cancer. This is almost a metaphysical transposition, when I know in *my* bones that something is very wrong with *his.*

Oracle of Delphi—the back story: For those who like to have their favorite myths decimated by hard evidence acquired by archeologists and geologists—, it appears that the story of the Oracle of Delphi is not 100% accurate.

The ancient story tells of vapors rising from the chamber in which the Oracle sat and her channeling the wisdom of Apollo while under the influence of these vapors.

She would recite these words and the petitioner would puzzle them out and go on his way. The words would determine what decisions were to be made. The decision often surrounded whether a king or city state should go to war or should flee before an incoming attack.

It is thought that the priestess was inhaling hallucinogenic fumes from the fissure of the earth.

Herodotus, the great historian, recorded some of these prophecies. One took place in 480 BC. Xerxes, the ruler of Persia, was returning to Greece to finish conquering the land. The Athenians went before the Oracle for guidance and asked what they should do in the face of this imminent threat. The seer said:

Await not in quiet the coming of the horses, the marching
feet, the armed host upon the land. Slip away. Turn your
back. You will meet in battle anyway....

She recommended flight before the army of Xerxes, which the
Athenians took to heart.

What is interesting about her answers, is that they were always
given in hexameter. The words have a poetic rhythm the same rhythm
that Homer used in writing the Odyssey.

Modern day geologists provide some commentary. They state it
is thought that the priestess was inhaling hallucinogenic fumes from
the fissure of the earth. That area of the world is earthquake country.
The tectonic plates of the earth's crust hit against each other in Greece,
and there is evidence that fumes underlying the Temple area could
indeed have arisen from a seam in the earth.

As to the elegance of the prose: there are ancient reports that
the priestess spoke in gibberish, that she always had male priests in
attendance who did the translation for her. This would explain the lovely
cadence of hexameter, as well as the sophisticated understanding of
political and military matters.

While the image of a priestess who is a seer and a conduit into
the knowledge of the gods is attractive, it may not have been true.

Of course, if a patient came before me and gave me a history of
illness and complaints that invoked a deep dread, if I were indeed
the Oracle of Delphi, I would have to answer:

Beware the pain in the belly, the scourge of the bowels; for
the grave doth wait for no man but takes its own when the
time is ripe.

At which point, a patient would rightly run screaming from the
room. Alas, we doctors do not talk like that.

Instead, we say, "It could be something serious. We need to do
more tests. Here, let me send you for an MRI." All the while, I am
modulating my voice and trying to keep the hysteria at bay.

dr. death

Isn't he supposed to tell me I had done the best I could?

Patients die. This is a tragic truism in the world of medicine. Usually the patients who die are elderly. Patients die from diabetes and kidney disease, or from alcohol abuse and liver failure, or from heavy smoking and lung disease. Or patients die from cancer.

As a physician, I take these deaths in stride. I try to provide comfort care as they lay dying. Patients often pass into a dreamlike state at the end. They are not fully conscious. I provide morphine for any pain, which may or may not hasten their entry into the final, dreamlike state.

But it is the deaths of patients who are too young that tear me apart. And it is the deaths of patients I thought I could save that keep me awake at night.

I talk about this to a friend who is a psychiatrist. I lose a patient, but I am not sure if I have made a mistake somehow. The psychiatrist, who is in his late seventies, reproaches me.

"Do you think you are such an excellent doctor that no patients of yours will die? That you never make mistakes? And the rest of us whose patients do die, who do make mistakes, are lesser doctors than you?"

I feel stunned. Isn't he supposed to comfort me? Isn't he supposed to tell me I had done the best I could? Instead, he chastises me for thinking I am better than other physicians.

It takes me a few days to realize that what he says is helpful. He tells me I am a member of the brotherhood of physicians. Physicians are human and fallible. He, too, has lost patients and blames himself. In fact, upon further reflection, I realize that psychiatrists are, in fact, at the epicenter of risk. They see patients who are depressed and suicidal. Psychiatrists always take the risk that a patient will kill himself or herself. And some will, no matter how skilled the practitioner is.

The book *Kill as Few Patients as Possible* by Oscar London, MD, internist, helps me cope with failures. He says that *when* (not *if*) a doctor makes a mistake that causes a patient harm or even death, the doctor should sit down at a desk, take out a Valium pill from the drawer, and call a lawyer. This very sensible, matter-of-fact approach somehow comforts me.

He also describes how "Dr. Death" sits quietly in the corner of each exam room, making notes on each patient, and adding a patient's

I reach out for a higher power: I send them to see a specialist or to the ER.

name to his List each time a doctor fails to order the appropriate test or defers on an X-ray.

For me, if I sense Dr. Death in the room, eager to claim a patient, I reach out for a higher power: I send them to see a specialist or to the ER.

Patients should never underestimate the self-flagellation of the physician. It is always in the background: *God willing, do not let me lose this patient.* The heavy responsibility to mediate with Dr. Death is the hardest part of doctoring.

the caduceus

The globally recognized caduceus is a symbol of medicine: the rod with two entwined snakes. The snake and scepter motif has origins that go back thousands of years.

A mention of the snake-arrayed scepter is made in the Hebrew Bible. Midway through the story of the Israelites crossing the desert of Sinai, led by Moses, the people are terrorized by poisonous snakes.

God tells Moses: 'Make for yourself a fiery serpent and place it on a pole, and it will be that anyone who was bitten will look at it and live.'

Moses made a serpent of copper and placed it on the pole; so, it was that if the serpent bit a man, he would stare at the copper serpent and live.

—Numbers 201:4-9

It is thought that this dated to around 1500 BCE. Just to be fair, the Hebrews probably adopted the notion of a snake entwined on a staff from familiarity with the major civilizations that surrounded them—the Babylonians to the East and the Egyptians to the West.

The snake has been venerated as a source of magic and of healing for millennia.

It is the Greeks to whom we owe the addition of wings to the caduceus rod. Around 800 BC, the Greek god of healing, Asclepius, was portrayed as holding a winged rod with an entwined snake. His fellow god, Hermes, was the one shown holding a winged rod with the double snake design.

In ensuing centuries, the rod of Asclepius was adopted by doctors in the Western world as the symbol of medicine.

Apparently, our American version of the caduceus arose through a small error.

Someone was told to grab an insignia for the US Medical Corps and apparently grabbed the wrong rod from Greek lore. This individual chose the double snake symbol, which was technically Hermes', instead of the single snake version, which was Asclepius'.

No problem, though. Either one is a potent representation of the power of snakes to invoke magic and healing.

CHAPTER NINETEEN

a lingering
medical mystery

*He is not getting better
despite aggressive antibiotic treatments and
dies after three days in the intensive care unit.*

Most patients I could take care of as a physician, I could name what was causing their symptoms: gallbladder; prostate; staph infection; diabetes.

Then there were the patients whose diagnoses escaped me. Something more exotic, something that required tests or imaging not available in our little community hospital. I would transfer these patients down the road to the specialists at the Big City Hospital. In nearly every case, these specialists there could name what was going on with these patients.

Sometimes, though, even the specialists were at a loss. Even they—with access to advanced testing and imaging—would sometimes fail to make a diagnosis.

Sometimes, a patient's diagnosis remains a mystery for years. It was only with the benefit of collecting additional data—more bits of the story—and with hindsight, that I could put together a likely explanation for his illnesses. Constructing a likely explanation for his illness gave me some comfort. It relieved me of the fear that I could have done something different, that I somehow could have saved him.

the football player

Craig Mason is a 15-year-old high school student. He is one of fraternal twins. He is handsome and athletic, the apple of his mother's eye. His father is inordinately proud of his athletic prowess. He plays junior varsity football in high school. Craig has a girlfriend who is pretty, nice, and smart.

His mother brings him into the clinic on a Monday morning. He has been running a fever all weekend and complaining of a headache. This morning, the headache becomes unbearable. He is sent from the clinic to the Emergency Room for evaluation.

Soon after arriving in the ER, he becomes confused and agitated. His fever is high—102 degrees. His headache is severe. These are all signs of meningitis, which is an infection in the brain. His girlfriend is by his bedside in tears. We call for a helicopter to take him to the tertiary care hospital. They arrive quickly and whisk him away.

Craig is treated right away with a potent antibiotic for what looks to be a bacterial meningitis. I call the Big City Hospital down the road and get daily updates from their pediatric specialists. A lumbar puncture is done to look for signs of an infection in the brain. The results are indeterminate.

He is not getting better despite aggressive antibiotic treatments and dies after three days in the intensive care unit. This is devastating not only for the family but also for the community.

Craig had gone swimming in a pond near their house.

The football team holds a memorial service for Craig with the entire community attending, including another football player with a broken leg. Apparently, Craig tackled him during practice ten days before and broke his teammate's femur. It takes tremendous force to crack a femur, which is the largest bone in the body. Apparently, Craig had run into the other player's leg by using his head as a ramming device.

I go to his funeral, along with the rest of the clinic staff. The mother is distraught. We give her a blanket with his name on it, in lieu of flowers. The twin brother is wooden. He is pale and shows no emotion whatsoever. The girlfriend is sobbing.

The mother comes to the clinic a few days after the funeral. She is clutching the memorial blanket we gave her. In fact, she carries it with her for every clinic visit thereafter, for at least a year. She says it comforts her somehow.

On a visit to the clinic six weeks after the death, the mother mentions that Craig had gone swimming in a pond near their house on the Friday afternoon the week before he got sick. He had done nothing else out of the ordinary. She mentioned the swimming episode because it was a happy memory.

I have always wondered what caused Craig to get so sick so quickly. We never got a diagnosis from the specialists. I finally put together the sequence of events that preceded his illness:

1. a head collision with another player, so hard he broke the other kid's leg;

2. a swim in a shallow, warm pond a few days later; and

3. the onset of a fever and an apparent infection of the brain within another two days.

A raging infection of the brain is called encephalitis.

I suspect he cracked a nasal bone in the collision and then picked up a deadly amoeba when he went swimming. There is an amoeba that lives in warm ponds. It is deadly if it crosses from the nose into the brain cavity. A cracked cribriform plate—the nasal bone that separates nasal passages from the brain—would offer an excellent passage for this deadly amoeba.

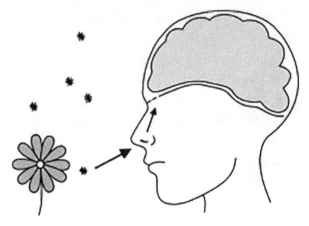

**Figure 10. Nasal cavity as portal
of entry for a deadly amoeba**

I was puzzled by Craig's death for years. It was only when I put together this retelling of the story and finally understood the above sequence of events that I reached some kind of closure.

Yes, the brain infection was swift and deadly. Yes, it was probably due to an exotic infection like the "brain-eating amoeba" instead of the ordinary bacterial meningitis for which he was treated. If so, then there was nothing I or the specialists down the road could have done differently.

what this patient taught me:

*That not every patient who presents with signs of meningitis
is easily diagnosed and appropriately treated. The story of
the head trauma and the swimming in warm water pond
emerged only weeks after his death. It is only much later that
the complexity of his illness became apparent.*

Medical Background: The "brain-eating amoeba" is officially known as Naegleria fowleri. The amoebae can cross from the nasal passages into the brain compartment. As its name implies, it destroys brain cells.

On average, it takes a few days for the symptoms to appear after nasal exposure. Symptoms include headache and fever, which then progress to confusion and seizures. Death usually occurs within two days.

CHAPTER TWENTY

lauren got sick: another lingering medical mystery

*A safe passage to the afterlife
required special spells along the way.*

L auren was my friend from medical school. She continued to be my friend throughout my years as a physician in Dry Lick. After being my consultant *par excellence* for decades, she was my go-to person when I needed to ventilate about patients, or I needed help with a diagnosis or treatment plan.

Then Lauren got sick.

The following is in her memory and a nod to the puzzling disease that took her life. This a tribute and memorial to her.

coffee with lauren

She was my constant companion for coffee klatches or for other equally exciting expeditions and adventures. We would go to the Gems and Rocks expos, to the fruit market, to the King Tut exhibit in Chicago.

Early on, she had a box of toys set aside for my little Becca, for when we came to her house. Lauren would come to Becca's overly-noisy birthday parties in my home or to our Thanksgiving dinners. She could take only so much of bonhomie and noise before retreating to the front porch and smoking a slew of cigarettes. She remained a serious smoker for the years I knew her despite the knowledge she gained about its dangers in medical school.

She was a pillar of support for me. We discussed cases every week at our coffee get-togethers, advising me from her vast knowledge of medical lore. She remembered everything we were taught in medical school.

Little Becca was growing up, and she got a baby brother. Lauren welcomed both children to her house. By this point in time, my older daughter was grown and in college.

We became experienced as primary care doctors, talking about the patients whose stories had amused us—or confused us. We talked about the patients we helped, which served a dual purpose.

The first reason was to counter the vast number of patients who did not need to see a doctor in the first place because they were not actually sick. They might have had a low-grade cold or were worried about something trivial.

The second reason was to counteract the number of patients we could not help because their illnesses were beyond the ability of doctors to cure. Patients like those who ended up dying of lung cancer or diabetes.

etchings and egyptian hieroglyphics

When we first met, Lauren showed me ornate etchings she had done of the brain and spinal cord. They were inspired by neuro-anatomy class. Who has not done etchings of the brain and spinal cord? She made it seem normal—decorating her house with them.

Later, she became deeply enmeshed in Egyptian studies, acquiring lots of books. She even taught herself hieroglyphics and the ability to write in it. She studied ancient Egypt and the *Egyptian Book of the Dead*. She explained to me that it gave one guidelines for how to travel from the land of the living to the afterlife over our coffees together. A safe passage to the afterlife required special spells along the way.

Lauren did etchings of Egyptian gardens and houses. Shadow boxes appeared: models of Egyptian houses with gardens. One shadow box showed a blue hippo standing next to a pond. These works of art were quite charming. She gave the hippo to Becca.

I knew Lauren had mental health issues. She told me she was on medicines for depression. Raised in an upper-middle class family, with an engineer father and a stay-at-home mother, who were not emotionally supportive of her. She also revealed that her mother had been unhappy. Apparently frustrated by a life that was limited to decorating and re-decorating houses and raising children. Her parents were puzzled by their brilliant, unsociable daughter.

Lauren displayed a deep knowledge of psychiatric meds.

For the first ten years I knew her, she hid her mental health issues from me.

Eventually, in bits and pieces, she told me she had been deeply depressed in her mid-twenties and that her psychiatrist had saved her life. He had started her on medicines that had made all the difference. She had been on these medicines, with occasional adjustments in dosage, ever since.

From her personal experience, Lauren displayed a deep knowledge of psychiatric meds. She was able to walk me through some doctoring dilemmas, informed by her intimate knowledge about these medications and of their side effects.

then lauren got sick

I had known Lauren for more than 25 years—since our first year of med school. We had continued to work and to meet for frequent coffees.

Then Lauren got sick. She developed weakness in her legs and numbness in her hands. She decided, somewhat arbitrarily, that her symptoms were due to leprosy. She had a patchy rash on her hands, with scant other reasons to land on leprosy as a possible diagnosis.

She had handled live armadillos years before, while volunteering at a zoo. She saw a local physician who gave steroids and exotic antibiotics for her out-of-left-field diagnosis. The meds did not help.

At the Sunday school class I taught, the kids were reading a story from the Bible about a priest sacrificing a bird and sprinkling its blood on a second bird that was set free: all this to cure someone of leprosy. Lauren came to the class and appreciated the reading of the story and the colorful illustrations the kids had painted of a bloodied bird flying free.

After working as a doctor for twenty years, Lauren could no longer work.

She still did not get better. Her condition worsened. After another two months, she could not walk anymore, her legs were so weak. She could not swallow normal food. Bed became her refuge with her cats for company.

After working as a doctor for twenty years, Lauren could no longer work.

Nothing helped. She was no longer on her psychiatric medicines. She decided their side-effects were dangerous.

Her psychiatrist had recently died, he had been in his 80s, so she no longer had him as her support. Her parents had also died recently. Grief surrounded her.

She started getting short of breath. She refused to see any doctors. She refused to get any testing. And she was adamant about avoiding hospitals. After training in hospitals for years, Lauren knew she could not tolerate the reality of being a patient in one. This may have been her depressive disorder talking.

I watched her waste away. I gave her low doses of pain medicines and of anxiety medicines. She said they helped. I would try to visit her, to read to her from her favorite murder mysteries. She said she was having trouble concentrating and appreciated being read to. Other than staying with her and keeping her company, there was nothing else I could do but be her friend.

Lauren would always weigh and measure her words, before this time, so that the sting was gone. In the past, she avoided hurting people's feelings.

But when she got sick, things changed. Her tongue became sharp. Not so much with me ... but with the helpers she had hired to clean the house. She would insist that things be placed just-so. I had never heard her utter a cruel word or be short-tempered before until her illness invaded her life.

Lauren became bedridden. The seven cats jumped in and out of her bed. They kept her company.

One morning, when the day help came, they found her still in bed, not moving. She had died overnight.

It's been many years since her death. I still miss her. I sometimes feel her with me at the clinic. I sometimes still consult with her about patient care. She is not there, of course, but I remember her (strong) opinions about this or that kind of patient, about this or that medicine to use.

As time has passed, I don't feel her presence as I did before. I think part of writing this book has been a way to still talk to her about the patients I've seen; to continue the discussions about whether we have done anything worthwhile, salutary, as doctors; to complain about the difficult patients.

She had written—in hieroglyphics—a prayer for an easy transition to the afterlife. I hope that gave her comfort as she journeyed over.

Medical Speculation: I always suspected some kind of cancer caused Lauren's strange assortment of symptoms. In writing this book, I have had the time to review her symptoms and to puzzle out what most likely caused her to get sick and die.

The most likely diagnosis? Small-cell lung cancer.

Lauren was always a heavy smoker; at least two packs a day for forty years. Her risk of lung cancer was high. It turns out that small-cell lung cancer can cause bizarre leg weakness and the other symptoms she developed.

Small-cell lung cancer is hard to treat, if not impossible. I suspect Lauren also thought it was a cancer that was causing her symptoms—and had calculated the cost of pursuing treatment for a cancer that was probably incurable.

Medical Background: Small-cell carcinoma can be hard to diagnose. The first symptoms may be unrelated to the lungs. Shortness of breath or cough may develop only years after other symptoms, such as muscle weakness.

How does cancer in the lungs cause weakness and wasting of the legs?

Cancer will trigger the immune system to develop antibodies. Their job it is to attack the invading cancer cells. Ideally, the antibodies are directed again the cancer cell itself.

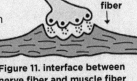

Figure 11. interface between nerve fiber and muscle fiber

It is thought in some patients with small-cell lung cancer that the army of attacking antibodies go astray. Instead of taking out the cancer cell, they attack other cells that carry similar-looking proteins. Specifically, they attack the complex where nerve signals get conveyed to muscle fibers. The muscle fails to receive the signal that says: "Time to contract." The muscle, without stimulation, begins to atrophy. It grows weak. The legs grow weak. The affected individual can no longer walk.

CHAPTER TWENTY-ONE

final thoughts

I practiced medicine in rural Kentucky for twenty years. I left only because my first grandchild was born. I moved 2,000 miles away to help take care of him. The grandmothers in town had shown me how important it was to share your life with a grandchild.

I am grateful to my patients for sharing their stories with me, for trusting me with their care. The trust and sharing gave me insights into people's lives I would have otherwise never gotten. Their stories have stayed with me all these years. They inform my understanding of how people get older and how people get sick. I am grateful for their wisdom, especially as I get older and as I need to deal with my own health challenges or those of my family.

I hope I have done justice to my patients and the other denizens of this little town. I hope I haven't said anything terribly unkind. Though I do have to admit, some of their antics were a source of great amusement to me.

Writing this book has enabled me to also wax poetic on the "Nature of Doctoring" and the challenges therein. Again, that is courtesy of the patients who have been my teachers all these years. It has also allowed me the opportunity to review how medicine has changed in the years since I was in medical school—the advances in genetics and in cancer.

Finally, this book has allowed me to write about my friend, Lauren. Her insights and opinions still echo in my mind. She was always one with strong opinions as well as a kind heart. This book is, of course, dedicated to her.

acknowledgments

The medical graphics were done by my younger daughter, Laura Davidson. The cover graphic is by Risa Aqua, an artist here in Denver.

My older daughter, Nina Snyder, edited and helped me put together the first rough draft of the manuscript. Judith Briles and her team (including Rebecca Finkel, who did the interior design), fine-tuned the manuscript and got it ready for publication.

Also, I want to thank my husband as well, for his quiet support.

about the author

Janet Tamaren, MD lived through the upheaval of the 1970s from Vietnam to the Women's Movement.

At age 38, giving in to a long-held ambition, she started medical school. She continued to raise a teenage daughter and had two more children while in training.

She worked as a family doctor for 20 years in rural Kentucky. She ran her own rural health clinic for ten of those years.

Retired now, she loves to write and travel. She also enjoys the company of her two grandchildren, especially when they are well behaved. Which is episodic at best.

Today, Janet calls Colorado home.

www.JanetTamaren.com